Advance Praise for Amy James's Knowledge Essentials Series

"Knowledge Essentials is a remarkable series that will benefit children of all abilities and learning styles. Amy James has taken a close look at the standards and testing around the country and developed innovative activities that support what's being taught at each grade while remaining sensitive to the fact that children learn at different rates in different ways. I highly recommend it for all parents who want to make a difference in their children's education."

—Michael Gurian, author of *Boys and Girls Learn Differently* and *The Wonder of Boys*

"Finally, a book about teaching young children by somebody who knows her stuff! I can (and will) wholeheartedly recommend this series to the ever-growing number of parents who ask me for advice about how they can help their children succeed in elementary school."

—LouAnne Johnson, author of *Dangerous Minds* and *The Queen of Education*

"Having examined state standards nationwide, Amy James has created innovative and unique games and exercises to help children absorb what they *have* to learn, in ways that will help them *want* to learn. Individualized to the child's own learning style, this is a must-have series for parents who want to maximize their child's ability to succeed in and out of the classroom."

—Myrna B. Shure, Ph.D., author of *Thinking Parents, Thinking Child*

"The books in Amy James's timely and unique Knowledge Essentials series give parents a clear idea of what their children are learning and provide the tools they need to help their children live up to their full academic potential. This is must reading for any parent with a school-age child."

—Michele Borba, Ed.D., author of *Nobody Likes Me, Everybody Hates Me* and *No More Misbehavin'*

KNOWLEDGE ESSENTIALS

FIRST GRADE SUCCESS

Everything You Need to Know to Help Your Child Learn

AMY JAMES

WITHDRAWN

CONTRA COSTA COUNTY LIBRARY

3 1901 04024 0998

JOSSEY-BASS

www.josseybass.com

Copyright © 2005 by Amy James. All rights reserved.

Published by Jossey-Bass
A Wiley Imprint
989 Market Street, San Francisco, CA 94103-1741

Design and composition by Navta Associates, Inc.

No part of this publication may be reproduced, stored in a retrieval system, or transmitted in any form or by any means, electronic, mechanical, photocopying, recording, scanning, or otherwise, except as permitted under Section 107 or 108 of the 1976 United States Copyright Act, without either the prior written permission of the Publisher, or authorization through payment of the appropriate per-copy fee to the Copyright Clearance Center, Inc., 222 Rosewood Drive, Danvers, MA 01923, 978-750-8400, fax 978-646-8600, or on the Web at www.copyright.com. Requests to the Publisher for permission should be addressed to the Permissions Department, John Wiley & Sons, Inc., 111 River Street, Hoboken, NJ 07030, 201-748-6011, fax 201-748-6008, or online at http://www.wiley.com/go/permissions.

Limit of Liability/Disclaimer of Warranty: While the publisher and author have used their best efforts in preparing this book, they make no representations or warranties with respect to the accuracy or completeness of the contents of this book and specifically disclaim any implied warranties of merchantability or fitness for a particular purpose. No warranty may be created or extended by sales representatives or written sales materials. The advice and strategies contained herein may not be suitable for your situation. You should consult with a professional where appropriate. Neither the publisher nor author shall be liable for any loss of profit or any other commercial damages, including but not limited to special, incidental, consequential, or other damages.

Readers should be aware that Internet Web sites offered as citations and/or sources for further information may have changed or disappeared between the time this was written and when it is read.

Permission is given for individual classroom teachers to reproduce the pages and illustrations for classroom use. Reproduction of these materials for an entire school system is strictly forbidden.

Jossey-Bass books and products are available through most bookstores. To contact Jossey-Bass directly call our Customer Care Department within the U.S. at 800-956-7739, outside the U.S. at 317-572-3986, or fax 317-572-4002.

Jossey-Bass also publishes its books in a variety of electronic formats. Some content that appears in print may not be available in electronic books.

Library of Congress Cataloging-in-Publication Data:

James, Amy, date.
   First grade success : everything you need to know to help your child learn / Amy James.
      p. cm.
   Includes bibliographical references and index.
   ISBN-13 978-0-471-46818-9 (pbk.)
   ISBN-10 0-471-46818-5 (pbk.)
 1. First grade (Education) 2. First grade (Education)—Curricula—United States.
3. Education, Elementary—Parent participation. I. Title.
   LB15711st .J36 2005
   372.24'1—dc22   2004021749

Printed in the United States of America

FIRST EDITION

PB Printing 10 9 8 7 6 5 4 3 2 1

*This book is dedicated to those whom I have taught
and those who have taught me.*

CONTENTS

ACKNOWLEDGMENTS

I would like to thank the following people for advising me on this book:

My mother, Cindy King, is a retired early childhood and reading specialist who taught kindergarten and first grade for thirty years. She assisted in establishing the transition program at her school district for children who are developmentally young.

My father, E. W. James, was an elementary school principal and elementary school teacher for fifteen years. He led the school district's efforts to serve children with special needs.

Gloria Hamlin, my supervising administrator during my teaching years, retired from Norman Public School after spending twenty-two years teaching math and eleven years as a middle school administrator. She directed the math, science, and technology departments.

Elizabeth Hecox is in her sixteenth year of teaching at Kennedy Elementary School in Norman, Oklahoma. She is an incredible classroom teacher, and the book is better because of her work with me on it.

Kim Lindsay is in her twelfth year of teaching elementary school in Dallas Public Schools and in Norman Public Schools. She was elected teacher of the year at Kennedy Elementary School for 2001–2002.

Holly Sharp taught English language arts for thirty years in five states and served as department chair for twelve years. She has written curriculum for Norman Public Schools and is an advisory board member for both the University of Oklahoma and Norman Public Schools.

The employees of Six Things, Inc., are a group of more than twenty current and former teachers who provide invaluable assistance on a daily basis. Anytime I needed help in any subject area, for any grade, their enormously good brains were at my disposal. This book series would not be possible without their assistance, and I am eternally grateful to them for their help.

Introduction

Ah, parenthood. You majored in it in college, right? Took all the high school parent preparation classes? Ha! If only these things really existed. Parenting may be the single most important thing you do, and you are expected to do it with hardly any preparation. But hey, that didn't stop you, did it? When your child was an infant, you read all the books. When your child entered the terrible twos, you rearranged your house. Preschool came and you researched them all. Now here you are at the starting line of what looks like a twelve-year race to achievement.

You may be asking yourself these questions: Is there a place for me in my child's education? Is a teaching certificate a prerequisite for helping with homework? What do you mean my child has to pass a test to advance to the next grade? Where is the closest boarding school?

Relax, calm down, and stay in control. I think we all realize that your home is probably the most important learning environment your child will be in and that parents are the most important teachers. You and the learning environment you create in your home need to accommodate your child's growth and increasing skill levels.

As a parent you are a primary caregiver, role model, and provider.

Your first grader looks to you as the final authority, the last word, and the smartest, strongest, and prettiest or most handsome person he or she knows. Enjoy it; it starts to wane toward the end of first grade. Learning environments are important. Whether your child is at school, at home, or in the car, the way you interact with your little learner will influence his or her abilities for a lifetime.

To effectively enhance your child's learning, you need to be constantly and consistently aware of your child's development over the years so that you can come to know his or her particular strengths, shortcomings, and areas of talent and natural inclination. (Be honest with yourself about the last part; not every little girl is a beauty queen and not every little boy is an athlete.) And just because you know one of your children does not mean you know them all. Children's minds differ substantially. Each child is his or her own person with a unique set of abilities. As you gain insight into your children's development, you can easily help them individually strengthen their abilities while also concentrating on areas of difficulty.

Life at home matters. An academically progressive home life is the key to effectively tracking your child's development as well as providing the opportunity to successfully apply knowledge. Creating the environment is about creating the opportunity to learn. The point is to bring the level of content and conversation in your daily life to the level that is in your child's school life. Home, your child's first learning environment, is the primary testing ground for new knowledge and skills.

Getting the Most from This Book

This book is a guide to creating an exceptional learning environment in your home. It contains curricula and skills unique to first grade presented in a way that makes it easy to put what you learn into practice immediately. This book serves as a tool to help solve the mystery behind creating a supportive, learning-rich environment in your home that fosters a thinking child's development while enriching his or her curricula. It contains dozens of mini–lesson plans that contain easy-to-use activities designed to help your child meet your state's learning requirements. An environmental learning section in each chapter tells you how to identify learning opportunities in the everyday world.

Chapters 2 through 4 give you some child development information to get you started. Teaching is about knowing the subject area you teach, but moreover it is about knowing the abilities of the students you teach. As a parent you can easily see the milestones your child reaches at an early age (crawling, walking, talking, etc.), but milestones are not always apparent in your six- to nine-year-old. These chapters explain the child development processes that take place during first grade, including what thinking milestones your child's brain is capable of and will reach in normal development during this time. In order for you to teach effectively, you will need to account for these developmental milestones in all topics and skills that you introduce.

Teaching is also about recognizing how different people learn and tailoring the way you teach to suit them. You will find out how to recognize different learning styles in chapter 3, which will help you implement the learning activities in the rest of the book.

Chapters 5 through 11 provide general subject area information for the first grade curriculum. The curriculum discussed in this book was chosen by reviewing all fifty of the state learning standards, the National Subject Area Association learning standards, the core curriculum materials that many school districts use, and supplemental education products. While there are some discrepancies in curricula from region to region, they are few and far between. Chances are that even if you aren't able to use all of the topical subject area units (such as social studies and science), you will be able to use most of them. Reading, writing, and math are skill-based subjects, particularly in first grade, and those skills are chosen according to specific child developmental indicators. It is likely that you will be able to use all of the information in those chapters. Each chapter provides learning activities that you can do at home with your child.

The focus of chapter 12 is understanding the social environment in first grade, including how your child interacts with peers and his or her social needs. Chapter 13 discusses how your child will demonstrate that he or she is prepared for second grade. The appendixes provide information on products that meet certain first grade learning needs.

You won't read this book from cover to cover while lounging on the beach. Hopefully it will be a raggedy, dog-eared, marked-up book that has been thumbed through, spilled on, and referred to throughout the school year. Here are some tips on using this book:

Do

- Use this book as a reference guide throughout your child's first grade year.

- Model activities and approaches after the information you find in this book when creating your own supplemental learning activities.

- Modify the information to meet your needs and your child's needs.

Don't

- Complete the activities in this book from beginning to end. Instead, mix and match them appropriately to the curriculum and/or skills your child is learning in school.

- Use this book as a homeschool curriculum. It will help with your homeschooling in the same way it helps parents that don't homeschool—it supplements the first grade core curriculum.

• Challenge your child's teacher based on information you find here. ("Why isn't my child covering ocean life as it said in *First Grade Success*?") Instead, look for the synergy in the information from both sources.

Use this book and its resources as supplemental information to enhance your child's first grade curriculum—and let's make it a good year for everyone!

Getting the Most for Your First Grader

1

No parent says, "Oh, mediocre is okay for my child. Please do things halfway; it doesn't matter." Parents want the best for their children. This is not a matter of spending the most money on education or buying the latest educational toy. It is a matter of spending time with your child and expending effort to maximize what he or she is being provided by the school, by the community, and at home.

Getting the Most from Your School System

You wouldn't think twice about getting the most bang for your buck from a hotel, your gym, or a restaurant, and you shouldn't think twice about getting the most from your school system. The school system was designed to serve your needs, and you should take advantage of that.

Public Schools

Part of learning how to manage life as an adult is knowing how to manage interaction with bureaucratic agencies, so it makes sense that part of this learning take place within a kinder, gentler bureaucratic system. This is a good introduction to working within a system that was formed to assist in the development of children's abilities. Schools are also a workplace—with a chain of command—and that is a good induction into the workplace your child will enter as an adult. To further your children's educational experience, you and your children will have the opportunity to meet and work with:

- School personnel: your child's teacher, teacher's aides, specialists, the school counselor, the administrator or principal, and others

- Extracurricular groups: scouts, sports, after-school programs, and community parks and recreation programs

- Parents: of children from your child's class or grade level, school volunteers, and parent–teacher organizations

Participation in your child's education is paramount to his or her success. Active participation doesn't mean that you have to spend hours at the school as a volunteer, but it does include reading all of the communications your school sends either to you directly or home with your child. Also, read the school handbook and drop by your child's school on a regular basis if possible. If you can't stop by, check out the school or class Web site to see what units are being covered, any upcoming events, and so on. Participation means attending school events when you can, going to class parties when possible, and going to parent–teacher conferences. If they are scheduled at a time when you are not available, request a different time. The school administrator or principal usually requires that teachers try to accommodate your schedule.

The single most important thing you can do to get the most out of your local school system is to talk to your child's teacher. Find out what curricula your child will be covering and how you can help facilitate learning. Does the teacher see specific strengths and weaknesses that you can help enhance or bring up to speed? The teacher can help you identify your child's learning style, social skills, problem-solving abilities, and coping mechanisms.

Teachers play a role that extends outside the classroom. Your child's teacher is the perfect person to recommend systemwide and community resources. Teachers know how to find the local scout leaders, tutors, good summer programs, and community resources. Your child's teacher may be able to steer you in the right direction for getting your child on an intramural team. Teachers are truly partners in your child's upbringing.

Your child's teacher cares about your child's well-being. Everyone has heard stories about having a bad teacher or one who was "out to get my child." If that's the way you feel, then it's even more important to have regular conversations with the teacher. Maybe his or her actions or your child's actions are being misunderstood. In any case, your child's teacher is the main source of information about school and the gateway to resources for the year, so find a way to communicate.

If you know there is a problem with the teacher that needs to be taken seriously, try the following:

- Talk to parents with children in the class ahead of your child. They may be able to tell you how the issue was approached by parents the previous year and they will have lots to tell about their experiences with teachers your child will have next year.

- Talk to your child's principal. This may result in your child being transferred to another class, so make sure you are prepared for that prior to making the appointment. Be willing to work with your child's current teacher prior to transferring your child. The less disruption your first grader experiences, the better.

- Talk to your local school administration center to see what the procedures are for transferring to another school. You will likely be required to provide transportation to a school outside of your home district, but if the problem is severe enough, it will be worth it.

No matter what, active participation and communication with your child's school is essential. It empowers you to:

- Accurately monitor your child's progress

- Determine which optional activities would enrich your child's learning experience

- Prepare your child for upcoming events, curricula, and skill introduction

- Share and add to the school learning environment

- Create a complementary learning environment in your home

- Spend time with your child

And just a word about the school secretary: this person knows more about what is going on in that building than anyone else. When I was a teacher, the school secretary always added to my and my students' success. The secretary is a taskmaster, nurse, mom or dad, and generally just a comforting figure in what can sometimes be a really big building. The school secretary always knows what forms to fill out, which teacher is where, what students are absent and why, when the next school event is, and how much candy money you owe for the latest fund-raiser. He or she is a source of lunch money, milk money, extra pencils, bus passes, and the copy machine. Get to know and love your school secretary.

Private Schools

On a micro level, participating in your child's education if she attends a private school isn't much different from participating if she attends a public school. Private schools have access to the same community resources. If you have a special needs child, the private school should work with local education agencies to see that your child gets the appropriate services. Through active communication and participation, you will derive the same benefits as parents whose children attend public school.

On a macro level, private schools are different from public schools. Private schools are governed not by a school board but by an internal system. This can be both easier and harder to navigate. Dealing with private schools is easier because the schools realize that you are paying tuition every month, so frankly they want to please their customers. Dealing with private schools is harder because they aren't accountable to the community for their actions nor are they governed by the same due processes as the public school system. Check out the school's administration hierarchy to see how decisions are made and what roles have been created for parent governance. Also, get to know the school's secretary.

To really be on top of things, it's a good idea to print a copy of your state's learning standards (see chapter 4) and familiarize yourself with the topics and skills that your state thinks first graders should learn. You can find a copy at www.knowledgeessentials.com. Compare the standards to those of your private school's first grade curriculum. If the curriculum is drastically different from the required state learning standards, your child will have difficulty passing the required state assessments. If your child's curriculum meets and exceeds the standards, your child will be well served by that school.

Private schools have the flexibility to incorporate religious elements or varied teaching philosophies that public schools can't provide. They are not subject to the separation of church and state requirements. Private schools operate without depending on community support (such as bond proposals); so as long as their tuition-paying constituency approves of their methods and the students who graduate from the programs demonstrate success, private schools can implement teaching methods at will that fall out of the mainstream.

Getting the Most from Your Homeschool Curriculum

A little power is a dangerous thing. You are homeschooling your child because you want more control over what and how your child learns and the environment in which he learns it. That is admirable, but don't be fooled. To a large extent, your child's natural ability to learn certain things at certain times will dictate the way you should approach any homeschool curriculum (chapters 2 and 3 explain this more fully). The best thing you can do when starting to homeschool your child is look at books on child development. Start with these:

- *Children's Strategies: Contemporary Views of Cognitive Development*, edited by David F. Bjorklund. Hillsdale, N.J.: Erlbaum Associates, 1990.

- *Piaget's Theory: Prospects and Possibilities*, edited by Harry Beilin. Hillsdale, N.J.: Erlbaum Associates, 1992.

- *Instructional Theories in Action: Lessons Illustrating Selected Theories and Models*, edited by Charles M. Reigeluth. Hillsdale, N.J.: Erlbaum Associates, 1987.

- *All Our Children Learning*, Benjamin S. Bloom. New York: McGraw-Hill, 1981.

You don't have to homeschool your child all by yourself or by limiting yourself to a particular homeschool organization's materials. Each state has some form of a regional education system with centers open to the public. At your public school system's curriculum resource center, you can check out curriculum materials and supplemental materials. Most of these centers have a workroom with things like a die press that cuts out letters and shapes from squares to animals to holiday items. Regional education centers often provide continuing education for teachers, so they usually have some training materials on hand. Look for information about your regional center on your state department of education's Web site. You can find a link to your state department of education at www.knowledgeessentials.com.

You can purchase homeschool curriculum kits designed to provide your child with a lion's share of the materials needed to complete a grade level. You can also buy subject area–specific curricula. It is important to ask the company that sells the curriculum to correlate the materials with your state's learning standards so that you can see which standards you need to reinforce with additional activities. You can find the companies that sell these kits at www.knowledgeessentials.com.

Using Supplemental Materials

You cannot expect any single curriculum in any public school, private school, or homeschool to meet all of the learning standards for the grade level and subject area in your state. Many will meet 90 percent of the standards and some will meet 75 percent, which is why there are supplemental materials. Schools use them and so should you. They are simply extra materials that help your child learn more. Examples of these materials include:

- Trade books. These are just books that are not textbooks or workbooks—in other words, the kinds of books, fiction and nonfiction, that you would check out at the library or that your child would choose at a bookstore. Trade books don't have to tell about many things in a limited number of pages so they can tell a lot more about a single topic than a textbook can. They give your child a chance to practice skills that she is learning. If you choose wisely, you can find books that use newly learned reading skills, such as compound words, blends, prefixes and suffixes, or rhyming. Sometimes these skills will be set in the context of newly learned science or social studies topics, such as weather, habitats, or your community. Many companies provide these types of books for sale, but the most recognizable one may be Scholastic, Inc. Appendix A lists some books that are really good for first graders.

- Software and the Internet. Schools choose electronic activities and content, such as educational software and Internet sites, and electronic components, such as Leapfrog's LeapMat, allowing your child to expand his content knowledge while implementing skills just learned. Supplementing what your child is learning at school with these resources helps him gain technology skills within a familiar context. If you choose wisely, such as starting with the software choices listed in appendix B of this book, you can sometimes enhance reading skills and/or supplement a social studies or science topic while your child learns to operate a computer—talk about bang for your buck.

- Other materials. Videos, photographs, audio recordings, newspapers—just about anything you can find that helps expand what your child is learning is a supplemental resource. Loosely defined, supplemental resources can include a wide array of materials; your newly trained eye is limited only to what you now know is appropriate for your child.

Now you know what we need to cover, so let's get to it.

First Grade Development

2

The journey begins. Good teachers base their activities on the developmental stages at which their students are performing. What is a developmental stage and why is it important?

The ability to learn is always related to your child's stage of intellectual development. Developmental stages describe how a child thinks and learns in different growth periods. These periods are loosely defined by age but are more accurately defined by behavior. They are important because children cannot learn something until physical growth gives them certain abilities; children who are at a certain stage cannot be taught the concepts of a higher stage (Brainerd, 1978).

The theory of child development that is the basis for modern teaching was formed by Jean Piaget, who was born in 1896 in Neuchâtel, Switzerland, and died in 1980. His theories have been expanded by other educators but stand as the foundation of today's classroom.

Piaget's Stages of Cognitive Development

Piaget is best known for his stages of cognitive development. He discovered that children think and reason differently at different periods in their lives, and he believed that everyone passes through a sequence of four distinct stages in exactly the same order, but the times in which children pass through them can vary by years. Piaget also described two processes that people use from infancy through adulthood to adapt: assimilation and accommodation. *Assimilation* is the process of using the environment to place information in a category of things you know. *Accommodation* is the process of using the environment to add a new category of things you know. Both tools are implemented throughout life and can be used together to understand a new piece of information.

Okay, did you assimilate and accommodate that? The main thing Piaget tells us is that that kids really can't learn certain information and skills until they reach a certain place in their growth that is determined by years and behaviors. Understanding Piaget's stages is like getting the key to Learning City because it is a behavior map that tells you what your kids are ready to learn. Let's define the stages, then look at the behaviors. Piaget's four stages of cognitive development are:

1. *Sensorimotor stage (0 to 4 years):* In this period, intelligence is demonstrated through activity without the use of symbols (letters and numbers). Knowledge of the world is limited because it is based on actual experiences or physical interactions. Physical development (mobility) allows children to cultivate new intellectual abilities. Children will start to recognize some letters and numbers toward the end of this stage.

2. *Preoperational stage (4 to 7 years):* Intelligence is demonstrated through the use of oral language as well as letters and numbers. Memory is strengthened and imagination is developed. Children don't yet think logically very often, and it is hard for them to reverse their thinking on their own. Your little angel is still pretty egocentric at this age, and that is normal.

3. *Concrete operational stage (7 to 11 years):* As children enter this stage, they begin to think logically and will start to reverse

thinking on their own—for example, they will begin to complete inverse math operations (checking addition with subtraction, etc.). Expressing themselves by writing becomes easier. Logical thinking and expression is almost always about a concrete object, not an idea. Finally, children begin to think about other people more—they realize that things happen that affect others either more or less than they affect themselves.

4. *Formal operational stage (11 years and up):* As children become formally operational, they are able to do all of the things in the concrete operational stage—but this time with ideas. Children are ready to understand concepts and to study scientific theories instead of scientific discoveries. They can learn algebra and other math concepts not represented by concrete objects that can be counted. Whereas every stage until now has continuously moved forward, this is the only stage where a step back occurs. As a teenager, your child will become egocentric once again. It won't be easy for you. Thinking and acting as if the world exists exclusively for him or her is cute behavior for a five-year-old; it is rarely cute for a teenager.

Unfortunately, only 35 percent of high school graduates in industrialized countries obtain formal operations; many people will not ever think formally. However, most children can be taught formal operations.

The graph on page 18 puts the stages in a clear perspective.

Developmental Goals for Six-Year-Olds

Now that you know the basics of developmental indicators, let's get down to the nitty-gritty of what can be expected from your new first grader. A six-year-old can/will:

- Follow two-step oral directions
- Listen attentively for ten minutes or more

Percentage of Students in Piagetian Stages

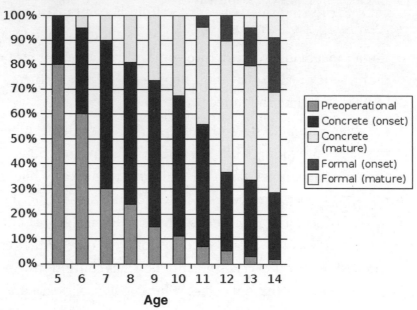

- Draw a picture of his or her whole self (not just a head but a head with a neck, a torso, etc.)

- Tell exactly how old he is and how old he will be next year ("I am six and a half years old; I'll be seven")

- Think logically some of the time

- Reason

- Understand the concept of cause and effect

- Exchange best friends and enemies easily

- Exhibit bossy behavior

- Become competitive

- Become moody

- Seek adult and peer approval

- Get upset when criticized

- Learn well through active involvement

- Continue to develop fine motor skills

- Manipulate small tools such as scissors

- Play board and card games

- Follow the rules

- Name colors

- Know his or her phone number and address

- Speak clearly

Your six-year-old's behavior while playing is a good indicator that he or she is beginning to develop concrete operational characteristics. Your child will engage in fantasy play less—for example, playing house is not as popular, there are fewer battles between Ninja warriors, and imaginary friends seem to go by the wayside. Your child may want to ride a bike, play team sports, or start craft projects instead. His or her attention span is still a little short, but you will see changes in what your child is paying attention to even if the follow-through is thin. Your six-year-old tends to develop stronger friendships but still needs his or her mommy and daddy.

A six-year-old child is being led along the path to independent behavior at school—being responsible for following rules, bringing lunch or lunch money, and taking things from school to home and back to school. This is not kindergarten; it is first grade. It is time for a little responsibility. Your six-year-old sees this as an opportunity for approval at home as well as at school. It is the perfect time to give him or her a weekly chore.

Developmental Goals for Seven-Year-Olds

Some first graders will turn seven during the school year. Here are some things you can expect from your seven-year-old. A seven-year-old can/will:

- Enjoy testing his or her own strength and skills
- Balance well
- Catch small balls
- Tie shoelaces
- Print his or her full name
- Reverse letters (*b* becomes *d*)
- Plan and build objects and do crafts
- Read often
- Identify the difference between left and right
- Know the days of the week
- Want to spend a lot of time with friends
- Enjoy rules, rituals, and routines
- Be interested in doing things correctly
- Begin to understand others' views
- View life in absolutes
- Enjoy being around younger children
- Expect to have accomplishments acknowledged

One of the first things you will notice as your child moves from six-year-old to seven-year-old behaviors is that he will become even less interested in fantasy play. Seven-year-olds are far more interested in projects or defined games—activities that they view as "real." Your child will begin to follow through on projects and find solutions to problems. Seven-year-olds understand rules and incorporate them into play.

You will notice that your child becomes less dependent on adults at this time and more dependent on his friends. As children become autonomous, friends and teamwork become really important factors for growth, self-confidence, and self-worth. Children begin to define themselves according to simple observations, such as "I am a fast runner." Unfortunately, this is the point at which self-doubt and self-consciousness can ensue.

Now, you may be thinking, Oh no! My child is all over both lists—and she is eight! Remember, children vary greatly. It is common to find a two-and-a-half-year difference in development among children. Six- to eight-year-olds who lag in specific skills often compensate by exceeding expectations in other areas of development. Don't worry. The best indicator of whether a child is in danger of falling behind is the rate of growth rather than an inventory of skills. If your child is making progress along the rough developmental continuum, don't be overly concerned about a few skills here and there.

First Grade Learning

3

If you write it on the chalkboard, they will learn it. Sound familiar? If you are lucky, it doesn't—but for a great majority of people it is exactly how they were taught and were expected to learn. Luckily, in most schools, education has come to embrace children with different learning styles.

Learning Styles

Learning styles define how your child learns and processes information. Education experts have identified three main types of learning: visual, auditory, and physical. When learning a new math concept, for example, a visual learner will grasp the material more quickly by reading about it in a book or watching his or her teacher solve a problem on the blackboard. An auditory learner will understand the concept if she can listen to the teacher explain it and then answer questions. A physical learner (also known as tactile-kinesthetic) may need to use blocks, an abacus, or other counting materials (also known as manipulatives) to practice the new concept.

If you understand that your child is a visual learner most of the time—that is, he is most comfortable using sight to explore the world—you can play to his strength and incorporate physical and auditory learning styles when appropriate. It isn't unusual to interchange learning styles for different subjects. An auditory learner can easily use kinesthetic strategies to comprehend new math concepts.

Studies have shown that accommodating a child's learning style can significantly increase his performance at school. In 1992, the U.S. Department of Education found that teaching to a child's learning style was one of the few strategies that improved the scores of special education students on national tests. Identifying your child's learning styles and helping him within that context may be the single most significant factor in his academic achievement. Each activity in the subject area chapters of this book lists variations that help you tailor the activity to your child's learning style. Look for the symbols by the name of each learning style and use these styles to tailor the activities to your child's needs.

Learning styles are pretty easy to spot. All you have to do is watch your child's behavior when given a new piece of information.

👁 Visual

Would you give your right arm to get your child to listen to you? Are your walls a mural comprising every crayon your child has held? If you answered yes, you have a visual learner. You may not be able to get your child to follow two-step oral directions, but she can probably comprehend complex instructions when they are written on the blackboard or listed. Diagrams and graphs are a breeze. Your child can retell complex stories just by looking at one or two pictures from a book. Why is your child seemingly brilliant on paper but a space case when listening? Visual learners rely primarily on their sense of sight to take in information, understand it, and remember it. As long as they can see it, they can comprehend it.

Technically there are two kinds of visual learners: picture learners and print learners. Most children are a mixture of both, although some are one or the other (Willis and Hodson, 1999). Picture learners think in images; if you ask them what sound "oy" makes, they will likely think of a picture of a boy or a toy to remember the sounds of the letters. These kids like to draw—but you knew that by looking at your walls, right? Print learners think in language symbols: letters, numbers, and words. They would think of the actual letters "oy" to remember the sound they make together. Print learners learn to read quickly and are good spellers right off the bat. They also like to write.

Auditory

Is your child a talker? Is total silence the kiss of death to her concentration? Auditory learners understand new ideas and concepts best when they hear and talk about the information. If you observe a group of kids, auditory learners are the ones who learn a tune in a snap just from hearing someone sing it, or who can follow directions to the letter after being told only once or twice what to do. Some auditory learners concentrate better on a task when they have music or noise in the background, or retain new information more accurately when they talk it out. If you ask auditory learners what sound "oy" makes, they will recall the sound first and as many words as possible with that sound almost automatically.

Kinesthetic

Does your child need to touch everything? Physical learners (also known as tactual-kinesthetic learners—*tactual* for touch, *kinesthetic* for movement) use their hands or bodies to absorb new information. In some ways, everyone is a physical learner. If you peek into a classroom, you will see the physical learner tapping a pencil, a finger, or a foot, or twirling her hair to help her concentrate. These kids can't sit still and they are in the top percentile for being diagnosed with attention deficit disorder (ADD).

Before you run to the doctor because your child can't sit still, carefully observe him over a long period of time. Is the movement productive? Does he absorb or block information when moving? If he prefers to feel things in his hands or performs steady movement when trying to concentrate, he is engaging in productive learning.

Physical learners enjoy hands-on activities, such as cutting construction paper, sorting objects with their hands, and building elaborate projects. When you ask physical learners what sound "oy" makes, they will think of the physical cues used by the teacher or the cues they used when learning, such as tapping, physically picking the letters out of the alphabet, or holding *o* and *y* blocks.

Cognitive Learning

Cognitive learning levels are another way that teachers describe how a child processes information. I hear you asking, "Wow, how much of this do I have to remember?"—and you know I am going to say all of it, but it is really important. Let's recap for a minute to see how all of this fits together.

First, you learned about developmental stages, the physical growth that needs to happen before your child can learn certain things. Second, you learned about learning styles, the way your child prefers to process information. Third, you are about to learn about cognitive learning levels, the levels at which your child knows, understands, and can use information that he or she learns. Piaget identified the developmental stages in the 1930s and 1940s. By the 1950s, a group of researchers got together, led by Benjamin Bloom, and created the cognitive learning taxonomy designed to help you understand the levels of learning that can occur with new information. Bloom is often considered one of the most important educational theorists of the twentieth century. He was a professor at the University of Chicago who was more than a brilliant teacher: he was a brilliant thinker. Bloom spent his career researching how thinking and learning happened in students of all ages. Bloom and his researchers broke down the learning levels as follows:

Level 1: Knowledge. The things you know—bits of information that you can memorize, such as the ABCs.

Level 2: Comprehension. The things you understand—knowing the ABCs and understanding that they represent sounds.

Level 3: Application. The things you can apply—knowing the ABCs, understanding that they represent sounds, and then sounding out a word.

Level 4: Analysis. The things you understand well enough to think about them in a new way—knowing the ABCs, understanding that they represent sounds, sounding out a word, and then figuring out what the word means.

Level 5: Synthesis. Understanding something well enough to apply it to a new situation—knowing the ABCs, understanding that they represent sounds, sounding out a word, figuring out what the word means, and using it in a new way.

Level 6: Evaluation. Understanding something so well that you can tell if it is being used correctly—knowing the ABCs, understanding that they represent sounds, sounding out a word, figuring out what the word means, using it in a new way, and then figuring out if the new way is right.

Check the Bloom's Cognitive Learning Levels table on page 28 for some specific key words and behaviors for each level. Getting to know the key words will help you determine how to ask your child questions in order to find out the level at which your child understands new information. Use the examples in the right-hand column of the table to ask questions that check for each level of understanding.

Bloom's Cognitive Learning Levels

Cognitive Level	Verb	Key Words		Examples
Knowledge				
Recalls data. Exhibits memory of previously learned material by recalling facts and basic concepts.	Remember	choose define describe find how identify knows label list match name omit outline recall	recognize reproduce select show spell state tell what when where which who why	• Defines terminology/vocabulary • Describes details and elements • Recognizes classifications and categories • Knows principles, generalizations, theories, models, and structures • Knows subject-specific skills, algorithms, techniques, and methods • Names criteria for using certain procedures • Spells words • Outlines facts, events, stories, or ideas
Comprehension				
Demonstrates understanding of facts and ideas by organizing, comparing, translating, interpreting, giving descriptions, and stating main ideas. Understands the meaning, translation, interpolation, and interpretation of instructions and problems.	Understand	classify compare comprehend contrast convert defend demonstrate distinguish estimate explain extend illustrate	infer interpret outline paraphrase predict relate rephrase rewrite show summarize translate	• Summarizes or retells information • Translates an equation • Outlines the main ideas • Summarizes instructions, facts, details, or other things • Compares and contrasts ideas • Explains what is happening • Identifies statements to support a conclusion • Classifies information

Bloom's Cognitive Learning Levels

Cognitive Level	Verb	Key Words		Examples
Application Solves problems in new situations by applying acquired knowledge, facts, techniques, and rules in a different way. Uses a concept in a new situation or unprompted use of an abstraction. Applies what was learned in the classroom into novel situations.	Apply	apply build change choose compute construct demonstrate develop discover identify interview manipulate	model modify operate plan predict prepare produce relate select show solve utilize	• Applies a formula to solve a problem • Uses a manual to solve a problem • Describes how to use something • Finds examples to help apply ideas, rules, steps, or an order • Describes a result • Modifies ideas, rules, steps, or an order for use in another way • Selects facts to demonstrate something
Analysis Examines and breaks information into parts by identifying motives or causes. Makes inferences and finds evidence to support generalizations. Separates material or concepts into component parts so that its organizational structure may be understood. Distinguishes between facts and inferences.	Analyze	analyze assume categorize classify compare conclusion contrast discover dissect distinction distinguish	divide examine function inference inspect list motive relationships take part in test for theme	• Troubleshoots a problem using logical deduction • Lists components or parts of a whole • Names the function of something • Makes a distinction between two or more things • Classifies or categorizes a number of things • Draws a conclusion • Lists the parts of a whole

(continued)

Bloom's Cognitive Learning Levels *(continued)*

Cognitive Level	Verb	Key Words		Examples
Synthesis				
Compiles information in a different way by combining elements in a new pattern or proposing alternative solutions Builds a structure or pattern from diverse elements. Puts parts together to form a whole, with emphasis on creating a new meaning or structure.	Create	adapt arrange build categorize change choose combine compile compose construct create delete design develop devise discuss elaborate estimate explain formulate generate happen imagine improve	invent make up maximize minimize modify organize original originate plan predict propose rearrange reconstruct relate reorganize revise rewrite solution solve summarize suppose tell test write	• Integrates training from several sources to solve a problem • Formulates a theory • Invents a solution • Constructs a model • Compiles facts • Minimizes or maximizes an event or item • Designs a solution, model, or project • Adapts something to create another thing
Evaluation				
Presents and defends opinions by making judgments about information, validity of ideas, or quality of work based on a set of criteria.	Evaluate	agree appraise assess award choose compare conclude criteria	importance influence interpret judge justify mark measure opinion	• Selects the most effective solution • Explains a selection, conclusion, or recommendation • Prioritizes facts • Rates or ranks facts, characters (people), or events • Assesses the value or importance of something

Bloom's Cognitive Learning Levels

Cognitive Level	Verb	Key Words		Examples
Evaluation (continued)				
Makes judgments about the value of ideas or materials.		criticize decide deduct defend determine disprove dispute estimate evaluate explain	perceive prioritize prove rank rate recommend rule on select support value	• Justifies a selection, conclusion, or recommendation

Adapted from Benjamin S. Bloom, *Taxonomy of Educational Objectives: The Classification of Educational Goals, by a Committee of College and University Examiners* (New York: Longmans, Green, 1956).

The Standards   4

Standards-based education came into the national spotlight over a decade ago. Communities and school districts previously made their own curriculum choices. For example, in one school district civics was taught in eighth grade and in another district it was taught in ninth grade, resulting in uneven and low test scores, because children were not taught the same subjects in the same grades but were tested on the same subjects.

The idea behind the standards reform movement is straightforward: when states set clear standards defining what a child should know and be able to do in certain grades, teachers and learners are able to focus their efforts and highlight particular areas in which they need improvement. Ideally, the standards show teachers what they need to teach by allowing curricula and assessments that measure performance to be aligned with the standards.

As with all reform movements, there are people who disagree with the idea of creating common learning standards. They primarily point to tendencies to simply "teach the test" and complain that the standards limit content breadth and community input. The real gripe may lie in the fact that education has always been a local issue. It is easy to fear change when you fear community values may be lost by standardizing state curriculum. Others believe that standards even the playing field. Before you form your own opinion, let's take a look at standards-based education.

Standards-based education lists content and skills that children need to learn at each grade level. Success depends on combining content and performance standards with consistent curriculum and instruction as well as appropriate assessment and accountability. This is the point where teachers and learners start to feel anxious. Everything sounds very official, particularly the accountability part. What does this language mean and what happens if children don't meet learning standards requirements?

Relax—there are no learning standards police patrolling our neighborhood schools, libraries, and bookstores. There are simply baselines by which the state determines eligibility for a high school diploma.

Let's start by defining learning standards.

Types of Learning Standards

Learning standards are broad statements that describe what content a child should know and what skills a child should be able to do in different subject areas.

Content standards are a form of learning standards that describe the topics to be studied, not the skills to be performed.

Performance standards are a form of learning standards that describe the skills to be performed, not the content to be studied.

Public school teachers must ensure that their students are taught the required content and skills because they are accountable not only to the students but also to their state, their school district, and their community for every child's performance on test scores. Private schools are accountable to their constituency with respect to student performance but not to the public. In fact, school requirements as well as teacher licensure are not as strictly monitored for private schools. The academically strong private schools institute internal standards that meet or exceed state expectations for public schools, but there are private schools that feel other aspects of child development, such as religious development, take precedence over academics. If your child attends private school, you must research the school to make sure it meets your expectations both academically and socially.

The use of testing to monitor classroom instruction is central to the theory of standards-based reform. It assumes that educators and the public can agree on what should be taught, that a set of clear standards can be developed, which in turn drive curriculum and instruction, and that tests can measure how well students perform based on those standards. There are two main types of standardized testing that your child will encounter:

1. Tests to determine individual student eligibility for promotion and graduation, college admission, or special honors. This type of testing has a long history. Examples include high school exit exams and college entrance exams, such as the Scholastic Aptitude Test (SAT), and the Advanced Placement (AP) test.

2. Tests that measure and compare school, school district, statewide, and national performance for broad public accountability. Increasingly, policy makers at the federal, state, and local levels want to identify ways to measure student performance in order to see how well the public education system is doing its job. The goals of this accountability approach include providing information about the status of the educational system, motivating desired change, measuring program effectiveness, and creating systems for financially sanctioning schools and requiring educators to receive more training based on the performance of their students.

It makes sense for you to make sure the content and the skills that you work on with your child match the content and skills that the state has identified for that grade level. Children will do better on the standardized tests when more learning standards match assessment, or test, requirements. Legislation is in place that requires states to align their learning expectations with their testing expectations. The disconnect came when federal requirements for learning standards preceded testing requirements. Many states took the opportunity to test for content and skills that seemed more important than the ones enumerated in the learning standards. States and schools are working under federal guidelines to make all of the content match in a few years.

Learning Standards Resources

Each state has created a document that describes what children are supposed to know and what they are supposed to be able to do at each grade level and in each subject area. You may wonder who writes the standards and why you should believe that these people know what is best. A lot of public school teachers have wondered the same thing.

You can rest assured that writing the state learning standards is a collaborative effort. Most states rely on input from experts who know about the grade level and subject area. These experts could include teachers, researchers, people from the education industry, and school administrators. As an endnote or a footnote, each document lists the people hired by the state to help write the final version.

You can locate the standards that apply to your child through your state Department of Education's Internet site, by calling your state Department of Education, or through the Internet at www.knowledgeessentials.com. There are several things you should read for:

1. *Content standards*: What topics will your child be studying?
2. *Performance standards*: What skills must your child develop by the end of the year?

3. *Resources*: What resources are designed to help teachers meet the learning standards? Can you access them?

4. *Correlation reports*: Does the state provide a listing of how the required textbooks and other materials meet their own learning standards? Your school district should also be able to provide you with this information.

As you read your state's learning standards document, you may notice that you don't always agree with what is listed for your child to be learning. Is there anything you can do?

If your child attends a public school, there is little you can do to protest the prescribed curricula, but you can certainly enhance the curricula through learning activities at home. If your child attends a private school, you may have greater influence over classroom activities (as a paying customer), but you will probably not get the curricula changed to meet your concerns.

If you teach your child at home, then you have as much control as you would like over your child's curricula. You undoubtedly have specific beliefs that have led you to decide to homeschool, and you can remain true to those beliefs while still covering the required curricula. Even if you don't believe the required curricula are entirely appropriate, the assessments required by the states and higher education institutions will be normed to the learning standards of the state in which you live. The standards are just the basics that your child will need to succeed in mainstream society. There are many more opportunities for learning across a wide range of subjects that can be totally up to you.

First Grade Reading

5

Teaching your child to read may seem like one of the great mysteries of life, but it isn't. Your first grader is either already reading or is certainly ready to read.

Reading is not a single skill. It is a set of skills and subskills. Teaching your child to read is pretty easy when you break it down into the proper steps and use activities that fit the way your child learns. The basic sets of skills that enable a person to read are decoding (sounding out words) and comprehension (understanding what the words mean). Each is comprised of a set of subskills.

Beginning of First Grade Reading Checklist

Students who are working at the standard level at the beginning of first grade:

____ Know words have meaning

____ Know letters make up words

____ Know all or part of the alphabet

____ Recognize familiar written words, such as their name

____ Recognize written words found in their daily environment

____ Imitate reading; make believe they are reading

____ Hold books and turn the pages

Decoding Skills	Comprehension Skills
Associates sounds with letters	Pays attention long enough to read
Names the letters of the alphabet	Holds important information and concepts in mind while reading
Maps sounds to letters of the alphabet	Gains information from reading
Segments a word into individual sounds	Understands components of language necessary to make sense of writing
Blends sounds together to make words	
Identifies sight words automatically	

Decoding

Decoding is the ability to sound out and read individual words. To do this, children must learn to:

- Associate sounds with letters. Matching sounds to letter symbols is the first step in reading. As children learn that words are created when the sounds and letters are put together, they begin to decode. Decoding, or sounding out, words will eventually become automatic, and automatic decoding is the key component to being a good reader.

Sight Words

Phonics skills first result in your child knowing a set of sight words, or words that are so common that your child immediately recognizes them without sounding them out. Some sight words ("I," "if," "he," "as") are obviously appropriate for first graders; others ("could," "know," "think," "where") are not. Most educators use the Dolch list of sight words for beginning readers. The Dolch high-frequency list was published by Edward William Dolch, Ph.D., in his book *Problems in Reading* (Garrard Press, 1948). The Dolch list of high-frequency words comprises 220 words—excluding nouns—that were common to the word lists of the International Kindergarten Union, the Gates list, and the Wheeler-Howl list—lists that were used in beginning reading programs in the 1940s. The Dolch list has held up over time as a reliable high-frequency word list for beginning reading programs. Some words are out of date but not many. You can find the Dolch list at www.knowledgeessentials.com.

Many students do not need extra practice with sight words, as they learn them by reading them repeatedly in context. The learning of sight words in isolation does not make a reader. Sometimes a student can read the words from a list and not recognize the same words in a book or story. Sight words are an important component of early reading, not the basis for it.

Your child will be expected to recognize certain sight words and to sound out one-syllable words. Not all one-syllable words are sight words. Sight words are determined by frequency of use as well as how difficult they are to read. One-syllable words are just short words that are naturally the first words your child should start reading.

- Combine sounds into words. The ability to identify and combine the sounds that make up words is also known as phonemic awareness.

This following table describes some important skills related to decoding words, where children can run into problems, and what you can do to help them along.

Decoding Skills	Having Problems?	Quick Tips
Rhymes and plays with sounds in words.	Has difficulty making rhymes or playing with sounds in words.	Rhyme, rhyme all the time; when you are in the car, near and far, rhyme, rhyme, rhyme.
Blends syllables and sounds together accurately to make a word.	Has difficulty putting syllables or sounds together to make a word.	Play a game where you clap every time you hear a syllable.
Separates a word into its individual sounds.	Has difficulty segmenting (or breaking down) words into separate sounds.	Sing songs that focus on sounds; for example, "Bingo was his name-O."
Knows sound-symbol correspondences and can sound out individual words, such as "know," "round," and "then." You can find a list of more words at www.knowledgeessentials.com.	Does not know sound-symbol correspondences and cannot sound out individual words, such as "ask," "from," and "has." You can find a list of more words at www.knowledgeessentials.com.	Read aloud to your child on a regular basis.
Decodes an appropriate number of words.	Isn't able to decode an appropriate number of words.	Crack the code, everywhere you go—sound out high-frequency words.
Has built a repertoire of words that he or she can read automatically—that is, accurately and rapidly without excessive labor or effort. These are sight words, but I would also include words of interest to your child. The sight words first graders should know are found at www.knowledgeessentials.com.	Struggles through decoding words and has not established a repertoire of words that he or she reads easily or automatically. The sight words first graders should know are found at www.knowledgeessentials.com.	Flash cards are the way to go. Buy a stack of index cards and some markers.

The following checklist can help you track your child's decoding skills:

Typical first graders can decode:	My child can decode:
One-syllable words	
High-frequency or sight words (such as "I", "am", "is")	
Simple compound words	
Words associated with individual interests	
Environmental words—for example, cereal boxes, road signs, toy packaging	

Decoding Activities

Try the following decoding activities with your learner.

TIME: 20–30 minutes

MATERIALS

- list of word pairs— some with the same beginning sound and some with different beginning sounds, such as "him" and "her," "before" and "after," "sit" and "sat," "open" and "close" (your list can be from school or words that your child had trouble with in other activities; if you don't have a list of sight words, you can find one that is appropriate for your child at www. knowledgeessentials.com)
- paper
- pencils

 Same Sounds

Learning happens when: you say each word set to your child and ask him if the beginning sound is the same. When the sound is the same, ask your child to write the letter that makes that sound on a piece of paper.

Variations: Try this activity anytime without the paper and pencil.

Ask your child to do a specific movement, such as jumping jacks or clapping, when he hears the same sound at the beginning of the words.

If your child does better when he sees things, make flash cards of the words so that he can compare and decide.

If your child likes to talk, ask him to tell you if the beginning sound is the same. Then ask him to tell you what letter makes that sound.

Mastery occurs when: your child correctly identifies most of the word pairs with the same sound for three days in a row.

You may want to help your child a little more if: he is not able to identify when the word pairs have the same beginning sound. If this is the case, you may want to greatly reduce the number of word pairs in the set that have different beginning sounds. After your child has identified some of these simpler sets, go back to the original list of word pairs.

2 | Sounds All Around

Learning happens when: you say a one-syllable word and your child tells you the beginning, middle, and ending sounds.

Variations: Say a one-syllable word and ask your child to tell you the beginning, middle, or ending sounds only.

- Take it outside. Grab two or three jump ropes and ask your child to use the ropes to create each letter of the word.
- After your child has identified the sounds, ask her to write down the letters that make each sound.
- Mix it up. Ask for the beginning sound of a word, then ask for the ending sound of the next word.

Mastery occurs when: your child is able to tell you the beginning, middle, and ending sounds of words for five days in a row.

You may want to help your child a little more if: she is not able to identify all of the sounds in more than one word in a row. Try asking her to identify just one or two sounds in each word. When she has done this successfully for a few days in a row, ask her to start naming all of the sounds in the word.

TIME: 20–30 minutes

MATERIALS
- list of one-syllable words (your list of words can be from school or words that your child has had trouble with in other activities; if you don't have a list of sight words, you can find one that is appropriate for your child at www.knowledgeessentials.com)
- paper
- pencils

3 | Name Game

TIME: 15 minutes

MATERIALS
- list of names
- paper
- pencils

Make a list of names of friends and family, TV shows, holidays, movies, or games. Make sure that some of the names have the same beginning, middle, or ending sounds.

Learning happens when: you say three or four of the names and then ask your child to tell you which ones have the same sounds (either at the beginning, middle, or end of the word).

Variations: Say each name individually and ask your child to write the letter that makes the sound he hears at the beginning, middle, or end of the name.

Read through three or four names. Then repeat them and ask your child to clap when you say words that have the same beginning sounds. If the words have the same middle sound, ask your child to rub his tummy when he hears the words that have the same sound. Ask your child to stomp if the words have the same ending sounds.

Flash cards are a good tool for visual learners. Lay out three or four cards for your child to look at and say the words on them aloud. Ask him to choose the cards with either the beginning, middle, or ending sounds you're looking for.

Ask your child to pick out the sounds that are the same and then add a word of his own that has the same sound.

Mastery occurs when: your child correctly identifies the names that have the same sound for a few days in a row.

You may want to help your child a little more if: he is not able to pick out the names with the same sound. Try giving him the names in pairs and ask him to tell you which pair has the same sound.

4 Color Me Happy

Write the letter that the color of each crayon starts with on a piece of paper, then place the crayon beside the letter. Put only one crayon beside each letter (don't put black and brown by the letter B; put one or the other by the letter B). Make a list of one-syllable words that use these letters.

Learning happens when: you say one of the words from your list. Ask your child to pick up the crayon that is beside the sound she hears. Ask your child to write all of the sounds she hears in the word on a piece of paper using the proper crayon color for each sound. Your child will be spelling phonetically— that is, writing letters that make the sounds in the word. Proper spelling is not a concern here.

Variations: Ask your child to write the word she hears and then draw a picture of something that the word makes her think of.

- Try this activity outside on a grander scale. Follow the same steps, but use chalk and the sidewalk as the crayon and paper.

- Use your list to make signs of each word. Flash the sign and say the word. Then remove the sign from sight and let your child write the sounds.

- Before your child begins writing all the sounds she hears, ask her to say them aloud to you.

Mastery occurs when: your child identifies the sounds that she hears at the beginning, middle, and end of the words for a few days in a row.

TIME: 20 minutes

MATERIALS

- list of one-syllable words (your list of words can be from school or words that your child has had trouble with in other activities; if you don't have a list of one-syllable words, you can find one that is appropriate for your child at www. knowledgeessentials.com)
- crayons or markers
- paper

You may want to help your child a little more if: she cannot identify enough sounds in the words to spell them phonetically. Try asking your child to write the letters that make the sounds she does hear. Work on the same list of words until your child can identify each sound she hears in the word.

5 Alphasounds

Learning happens when: you and your child sing the ABC song, but instead of singing the letters, sing the sounds that they make.

While you're singing, pick out certain sounds (such as the vowels) and have your child add an action, such as touching his nose or patting his tummy, when he hears the appropriate sound.

Write the sounds in alphabetical order, then read them while singing (for example, buh, cuh, duh, ehhh, eff, juh).

Try clapping the rhythm while you're singing the sounds of the letters. Use words that all start or end with the same letter.

Mastery occurs when: you and your child can sing the alphabet sounds in the ABCs melody.

You may want to help your child a little more if: he has trouble singing all of the alphabet sounds. Try writing the sounds as suggested for visual learners, reading them, saying them, saying them to a beat, then singing them.

6 | Looks Like–Sounds Like

Learning happens when: you choose a letter of the alphabet and write it on the paper. Ask your child to name the letter. Talk to her about the letter—what it looks like and what it sounds like. The name of the letter makes a sound that the letter makes. Brainstorm all of the words that make that sound. Ask your child to find pictures of things with the same sound, then cut and glue the pictures on the paper.

Variations: Try this activity with each letter in the alphabet. Ask your child to find pictures that have that sound at the end of the word. (This is difficult and you will need to help your child.) Ask her to find pictures that have a blended sound at the beginning or end of the word. (Blended sounds include: bl, br, ch, gr, st, th, wr.) Make sure you spend time on what the blend looks like and sounds like.

- Go for a walk in your neighborhood and ask your child to point out things that have the same sound as the letter.

- Cut out the letter from a large sheet of poster board and have your child paste the pictures on the letter shape. It makes a good visual reminder of what she is working on.

- Listen to a simple song. Ask your child to pick out words that contain the sound of a specific letter.

Mastery occurs when: your child finds pictures of objects or actions that represent the sound of the letter on the paper.

You may want to help your child a little more if: she cannot find pictures of objects or actions that represent the sound of the letter on the paper. Try the activity again, but this time choose the first few

Time: 25 minutes

Materials
- magazines (or sales circulars, catalogs, or newspapers)
- rounded-edge scissors
- nontoxic glue
- large sheet of construction paper (or poster board, cardboard, or large paper bag)
- crayons or markers

pictures with your child. If your child chooses to follow her own path by finding random pictures or those that are grouped according to a theme of her own liking, then try the activity again, but this time talk to your child about the importance of following directions. If she continues to choose randomly grouped pictures, you may need to spend more time identifying the letter by name, sight, and sound.

7 | Sounds Like–Looks Like

Time: 20 minutes

Materials
- paper (or a paper bag or anything with space for drawing)
- crayons or markers

Learning happens when: you divide the paper into sections (for example, fold a square piece of paper into four sections, then unfold) and put the same letter at the top of each section. You may vary writing the letter in uppercase and lowercase. Talk about the sounds that the letter makes. Brainstorm words that begin with that letter. Ask your child to draw a picture of something that starts with the letter in each section.

Variations: Try this activity with each letter in the alphabet.

Instead of drawing things that start with that letter, ask your child to find small items in the house that start with that letter and place them in the boxes on the paper.

Ask your child to draw pictures that have that sound at the end of the word. Ask him to draw pictures that have a blended sound at the beginning or end of the word. (Blended sounds include: bl, br, ch, gr, st, th, wr.) Make sure you spend time on what the blend looks like and sounds like.

Instead of asking your child to draw pictures, choose a song, a poem, or a tongue twister that uses that letter's sound repetitively. When doing this variation, make sure that you start out with only a few letters a week.

Mastery occurs when: your child draws pictures with the proper sounds in them each time.

You may want to help your child a little more if: he can't decide what to draw. Try brainstorming things to draw with him. If that doesn't work, ask your child to find pictures that start with the sound and draw his own pictures by remembering the pictures that he found. If your child draws a picture that doesn't represent the letter, ask him to tell you what he drew. Is the object moving or performing an action that starts with the proper letter? If not, talk to your child about the sounds that he is hearing. Write the letter that is at the beginning of the picture's name beside the letter that your child was supposed to relate to his drawing. Ask your child to draw a new picture either now or at a later time. (Keep the paper he has been working on to review when you do revisit this activity.)

8 Color Time!

Learning happens when: you ask your child to color a picture in a coloring book. Look at the picture with her. Pick out a feature of the picture (if there are multiple figures in the drawing) and say its name. What sound does it start with? Name the sound and the letter that makes that sound. Write the letter that makes the beginning sound under the picture. Let your child continue on her own.

Variations: Write the letter that makes the ending sound under the picture.

TIME: 20 minutes

MATERIALS
- coloring book
- crayons or markers

✋ Pick an activity going on in the picture and ask your child to act it out. Then talk about what letter the activity starts with and the sound the letter makes.

👁 Look at the picture with your child and find other things that start with the same letter and sound.

👂 Talk with your child about other things on the page that start with the same sound. Ask her to find those things and say them aloud. Circle them on the page.

Mastery occurs when: your child writes the letter that makes the beginning sound of each picture that she colored.

You may want to help your child a little more if: she was unable to identify the letter that makes the sound at the beginning of the word for each picture. Then try finding other pictures that begin with the sound with which she is having the most trouble. Repeat the activity. You may need to write the alphabet on a piece of paper for your child to look at.

Your child may consistently identify a middle or ending sound. Try repeating the activity and talking about beginning sounds. What does beginning mean? What other things are at the beginning?

9 | Pick It!

Spend some time on your own choosing several pictures and gluing them on the paper, one picture per sheet (or just draw a picture on each piece of paper). Then write two words underneath the picture: one that matches the picture and one that is slightly different (for example, "sun, bun" written under a picture of a sun). Do this with each picture that you find or draw. It helps (particularly when your child is just beginning to decode) if you use pairs of words that only have one sound that is different (for example, far, car; toy, boy; road, toad).

Learning happens when: you ask your child to look at the picture and either point to the word or circle the word that matches the picture. Let your child read his answers back to you.

Variations: Write words with very different sounds under each picture. Write three words under each picture.

✋ When making the sheets up, use things that are around the house or in your child's room. Ask him to find the object and match the word to it.

👁 Ask your child to help you make the pictures and write the words.

👂 Say each word or ask your child to say each word before he picks the right word.

Mastery occurs when: your child correctly identifies all or a majority of the words for each picture.

You may want to help your child a little more if: he is unable to identify many of the words that match the pictures. Try reviewing the pictures with him and repeating the activity at a later time. If the problem continues, place the pictures that your child is having trouble with in other activities and concentrate on a set of five or ten words at a time until he has mastered them and the sounds that are in the words.

TIME: 45 minutes

MATERIALS
▪ pictures (from a catalog, magazine, newspaper, coloring book, or hand drawn)
▪ nontoxic glue
▪ rounded-edge scissors
▪ paper (or poster board, cardboard, or index cards)
▪ crayons or markers
▪ pencils

10 Flash!

Time: 30 minutes

MATERIALS
list of sight words
(your list can be from
school or words that your
child had trouble with in
other activities; if you
don't have a list of sight
words, you can find one
that is appropriate for
your child at www.
knowledgeessentials.com)
index cards (or paper,
cardboard, or poster
board cut into squares)
crayons or markers

Write one word on each of the cards.

Learning happens when: you show the words to your child one at a time and she tells you what the word says.

Variations: Make new sets of flash cards with progressively harder words in them each time your child masters an old set.

Place the cards in front of your child. Ask her to touch the card that shows the word you say.

Ask your child to help you make the cards.

Work on blends with your child. Make sets of flash cards with single letters or blended sounds in them and move on to simple sight words when your child has mastered the letters.

Mastery occurs when: your child can tell you what's written on each one of the cards for five days in a row.

You may want to help your child a little more if: she cannot recognize the words after seeing them many times and being prompted. Try going back to the letter and blended-sound flash cards and make sure your child has mastered those before coming back to this activity.

11 Magnasounds

Learning happens when: you say one of the words to your child and ask him to find the letter that makes the sound at the beginning of the word. Ask him to place the letter magnet that makes that sound on the refrigerator.

Variations: Ask your child to find the letter that makes the sound at the middle or the end of the word.

TIME: 20 minutes

Variations: Ask your child to find the letter that makes the sound at the middle or the end of the word.

Instead of using the alphabet letters, ask your child to find something else in the house that starts with that letter and bring it to you.

Get a few extra sets of alphabet letters and spell out three simple words that look alike (for example, cat, hat, bat). Then say one of the words and have your child pick it out of the three.

Select a letter magnet and place it in the middle of the refrigerator. Ask your child to say the letter, the sound it makes, and a word that starts with that sound.

MATERIALS

■ list of one-syllable words (your list can be from school or words that your child has had trouble with in other activities; if you don't have a list of one-syllable words, you can find one that is appropriate for your child at www. knowledgeessentials.com)

■ set of alphabet magnets

■ refrigerator (or other magnetic surface)

Mastery occurs when: your child correctly identifies all of the sounds in the one-syllable words that you say to him.

You may want to help your child a little more if: he is not able to identify all of the sounds in more than one word in a row. Try asking him to identify just one or two sounds. When he has done this successfully for a few days in a row, ask him to start finding all of the sounds in the word.

12 Speedy Sounds

Learning happens when: you write each letter of the alphabet on a separate piece of paper and arrange them face up on the floor in alphabetical order. Designate a starting place, then say a word, and ask your child to run to the first letter of the word. Ask her to either pick up the letter and bring it back to the starting point or "tag" it and run back to the starting point.

Time: 30 minutes

MATERIALS

▪ paper

▪ markers

▪ list of one-syllable words (your list can be from school or words that your child has had trouble with in other activities; if you don't have a list of one-syllable words, you can find one that is appropriate for your child at www. knowledgeessentials.com)

Variations: Ask your child to run to the letter that makes the sound at the middle or end of the word.

✋ Ask your child to run to the letters that make the sounds at the beginning and end of the word or the letters that make the sounds at the beginning, middle, and end of the word.

👁 Ask your child to help you write the letters on index cards and arrange them on the floor.

👂 When your child finds the letter that the word starts with, have her pick it up and say the letter and the sound it makes.

Mastery occurs when: your child chooses the letters that make the proper sounds for all of the words on the list.

You may want to help your child a little more if: she has trouble picking out the sound at the beginning, middle, or end of the word. Try making a single sound and asking your child to find the letter that makes that sound.

13 Sort the Sound

Time: 30 minutes

MATERIALS

▪ pictures (or photos that can be touched)

▪ rounded-edge scissors

Cut pictures out of magazines, catalogs, or newspapers, making sure there are at least two groups of several pictures that start with the same sound.

Learning happens when: you mix up the pictures, then ask your child to sort them according to beginning, middle, or ending sounds.

Variations: You may want to ask your child to name the picture and write down the beginning sound that he hears.

👋 Use real, manipulative objects—cherries, checkers, or chocolate—instead of pictures. Time to clean the room or do some yard work? Ask your child to sort and group things in his room or in the yard by a sound, and ask him to explain the groupings to you. Do all of these things start with the same sound, end with the same sound, or have the same sound in them?

👁 Instead of using pictures, ask your child to draw specific things and write the beginning letter, ending letter, or vowel sound that goes with each picture.

👂 Ask your child to "read" the pictures—saying each sound slowly and telling you the beginning, middle, and ending sounds of each picture.

Mastery occurs when: your child can decode what he has properly sorted and read all of the sounds to you.

You may want to help your child a little more if: he is not able to sort the pictures by sounds. Try reducing the number of pictures to pairs and start with just two pairs that are easily matched. It helps to use pictures that match word lists that he has been working on with you or at school. Build up the number of pictures as he is successful.

14 | Quiz Show

Learning happens when: you say the words to your child one at a time and ask her to tell you the sounds that she hears at the beginning, middle, or end of the word. Give your child a set time to answer and ask her to ring the bell before answering. Make sure your child waits to be called on instead of ringing and shouting

TIME: 20 minutes

MATERIALS
■ list of one-syllable words (your list can be from school or words that your child has had trouble with in other activities; if you don't have a list of one-syllable words, you can find one that is appropriate for your child at www.knowledgeessentials.com)
■ bell (or something that can be used as a buzzer to "ring in")

the answer. As the host of your in-home game show, you can play it up as much as you want—introducing your child, offering small prizes, and the like.

Variations: Vary the amount of time you give your child to answer.

Try having your child perform a specific movement instead of buzzing in when she knows the sound.

Instead of telling you the sounds she hears, have your child write out the sounds on cards and hold them up.

Ask your child to "sing in" with a line from a favorite song. This is fun for kids who like to hear things and do things, so it is perfect for both kinesthetic and auditory learners.

Mastery occurs when: your child rings in with the proper answer more than once.

You may want to help your child a little more if: she is unable to perform in the game show format. Try quizzing your child one on one until she is ready to follow game rules while decoding.

Comprehension

Learning to read words isn't all there is to learning to read—it doesn't do much good for your child to read words unless he or she understands their meaning. Comprehension means understanding what you read. Understanding has several components: language, attention, and memory.

Language

You already know that decoding is a crucial component of reading, but you may not know that children's ability to sound out words directly affects their ability to comprehend materials that they have read.

Children who decode words well are more likely to understand what the author means.

Yet there is more to understanding language than just being able to sound out words. Children have to learn about different kinds of sentences and certain punctuation rules to understand how the words are grouped and what they mean. Your child is just now learning reading rules that you take for granted—like reading from left to right and top to bottom. Reinforcing these comprehension skills can be as easy as following the sentences with your finger that you read aloud to your child, then asking your child to do this.

Attention

It takes a lot of mental energy to read. As reading material becomes longer, more complex, or more removed from everyday context, your child exerts more energy to comprehend the text. Mental energy is especially taxed if a child uses too much effort decoding words.

Paying attention enables your child to read in steps, which helps her remember what she is reading. The steps include looking at the pictures on the page as well as at graphic organizers, such as headings, titles, and words printed for effect, such as bold or colored text. Your child will then look at the words in a step that evolves into skimming or "prereading." Looking at the words to see if there are a lot of them, how many big words there are, and if there is any change in the print (italics or indentions) is the first stage of skimming. You don't really have to teach this; it just sort of happens as children actively try to pay attention to and understand the things that they are reading. The more interesting they find the materials, the more likely they are to try to absorb everything on the page.

Attention is required to pick out the most important details in passages. As children process information, they filter out the text that isn't important. While they do this, they are thinking about all of the pieces of information and concepts to understand and remember in their reading material.

Memory

Memory, the mind's hard disk, is essential in helping children comprehend as they read. It enables them to make associations between prior knowledge and new information, and to remember that same information at a later time. As children read, they must hold important information and concepts in their minds. They must process words, sentences, and paragraphs together in order to gain full meaning—all while calling up relevant information they already know.

Reading is no small trick, and memory plays a key role in it. Luckily, as we all know, children remember everything—and tend to repeat it at the most inopportune times. Channel your sponge's memory toward learning and have him or her reading for enjoyment and information as often as possible.

Higher-Order Cognition

Higher-order cognition is a fancy way of saying that your child is able to think through and apply the information that he or she just read on the different cognitive learning levels. These levels (Bloom's cognitive learning levels) are described in chapter 3 and can be applied to reading through the following categories:

Knowledge: Does your child know what she just read well enough to repeat it back to you?

Comprehension: Can your child state the main idea of the passage or story that he just read?

Application: Can your child apply what she read to something with which she is familiar?

Analysis: Is your child able to compare and contrast information that he has read?

Synthesis: Can your child predict the outcome of a story or make up a different ending to it?

Evaluation: Is your child able to discuss her opinion of what she read or the choices that she would have made to complete the story?

The ultimate goal of reading is to understand information. When children read for information, their ability to fully comprehend materials becomes really important. As they get older, good reading skills become the foundation for success in all areas.

The following table describes some important skills that enable reading comprehension, some problems your child might encounter, and some quick tips on how you can help.

Comprehension Skills	Having Problems?	Quick Tips
Easily holds information in his mind while reading further.	Forgets the beginning of a passage by the time he gets to the end.	Read a story; draw a picture. Ask your child to draw what he heard or read immediately after the story ends.
Is able to store information and then call it up sometime after reading.	Has a hard time remembering and repeating information after reading new text.	Use pictures, titles, and other graphic organizers to remind your child of what she has read.
Decodes new words easily so that reading is smooth and fluent.	Decoding is difficult, making reading choppy and hard.	Sound off—or out! Sound out words every chance you get, not just while reading books.
Is able to grasp the concepts involved in his readings.	Finds it hard to understand new concepts when reading.	Encourage reading in areas of interest, especially areas in which your child has prior knowledge.

Comprehension Activities

Try the following comprehension activities with your learner:

1 Scrambled!

TIME: 30 minutes

MATERIALS
- list of simple sentences
- index cards (or paper, cardboard, or poster board)
- markers (or pencils or crayons)

Using the list of simple sentences, write each word on a separate card. Group the cards into stacks according to the sentence they make.

Learning happens when: you mix up one stack of cards and give them to your child. Read the words in the sentence out of order (for example, ball up pick the). Ask your child to put the words in an order that makes sense (Pick up the ball). Repeat this activity with the rest of the sentence stacks.

- Kinesthetic learners like this activity just the way it is. Moving the word cards around to make sentences satisfies their need to move, and the movement is tied to learning.

- Read the mixed-up sentence to your child and ask him to write the words in the proper order. (This is a higher-level skill, and you should not expect your child to master this until the fourth quarter of first grade.)

- Read the mixed-up sentence and ask your child to read the words as he puts them in the correct order.

Mastery occurs when: your child puts the word cards in the proper order each time you say a scrambled sentence.

You may want to help your child a little more if: he is not able to put the word cards in the proper order. Try making up two- and three-word sentences, building up to a simple sentence with more words. If that is still too difficult for your child, pick one word at a time out of the word cards, and ask him to tell you the word and then use the word in a sentence. Write your child's sentence on the back of the card.

2 | The Five W's

Learning happens when: you read an unfamiliar story to your child. Read the book straight through without stopping to talk about it. When you are finished reading, ask your child Where? What? When? Why? and How? questions about the story.

TIME: 30 minutes

MATERIALS
storybook (one not familiar to your child)

Variations: Try this activity with factual text, such as an appropriate newspaper story. Try this activity with TV shows or movies.

- Go out for the day, explaining to your child ahead of time that at the end of the day you'll be talking about everything the two of you did. Go out for breakfast, go grocery shopping, call up a relative and chat, and let your child pick a few activities. Then ask her questions about the day.
- Give your child a short story to read and then ask the questions.
- Try singing a song that has a story to it, such as "Mary Had a Little Lamb," then asking the questions.

Mastery occurs when: your child can correctly answer all of the questions you ask.

You may want to help your child a little more if: she cannot correctly answer all of the questions you ask. Try stopping in the middle of the story and asking questions before continuing. You may need to stop several times to ask questions before building up to asking all questions at the end of the story.

3 | Swallowed First?

TIME: 15 minutes

MATERIALS
- "There Was an Old Lady Who Swallowed a Fly" (book or song)

Find the words to the song "There Was an Old Lady Who Swallowed a Fly" at www.knowledgeessentials.com or pick up a copy of the book from your local library.

Learning happens when: you sing the song or read the book with your child. Ask him sequential questions (for example, What happened first? What did she swallow second?). Follow up with comprehension questions focusing on details that don't depend on knowing the order in which the events happened (for example, Why did she swallow that?).

Variations: Mix up your chronological questions (for example, What happened fourth? What happened first?). You can also combine comprehension-based questions with chronological characteristics (for example, What caused her to swallow the second thing?).

✋ Ask your child to use objects that represent things in the book/song/poem to answer your questions. You can ask him to do things like pick up the fourth thing the old lady swallowed, or give your child three things that the old lady swallowed and ask him to put them in the order in which they were swallowed.

👁 Ask your child to write out a list of what the old lady swallowed first, second, and so on.

👂 Play the song for your child and shut it off right before the part about what the old lady swallowed. Ask him to fill in the blanks.

Mastery occurs when: your child can answer the questions accurately.

You may want to help your child a little more if: he cannot answer the questions accurately. Try making a list of the things the old lady swallowed and let your child look at the list while you ask the chronological questions.

4 Check It Out!

Learning happens when: you take your child to the library (not the bookstore, the library) to let her choose books to read. Let your child choose the books by looking at the cover and thumbing through the book. Ask her what she thinks the book is about based on the title, the picture on the cover, the pictures in the book, and the way the words are written (is it a large, fun font?). Does your child think the book will be funny or sad? Is the book about real things (people or animals), or is the book a fantasy (fairy tale, talking animals, etc.)? Check out the books that your child picks out and then have her read them at home. Ask her what she thinks each book is about before reading it, then compare what the book was really about to what your child thought it was going to be about. Was it an accurate prediction?

Variations: Ask your child to pick out a certain kind of book, such as fantasy or realistic fiction, based on the graphic organizers (for example, titles, headings) and pictures.

- Try this activity with a board game your child hasn't heard of before. Let her take a look at the picture on the box, read the descriptions, and look at the pieces. Ask her opinion of the game and then play it with her. Was the opinion appropriate?

- Try this activity with videos.

TIME: 60–90 minutes

MATERIALS
- library card

🦻 If your child does better when she listens to things, use books on tape, or record the books yourself. Let your child listen as she follows along with the book.

Mastery occurs when: your child accurately predicts in a general way what the books will be about.

You may want to help your child a little more if: she is not able to predict what the books are about. Try picking out a sequel or one of a series of books with which you know your child is familiar, such as *Arthur*, *Clifford the Big Red Dog*, *Curious George*, or *Frog and Toad*. Show the book to your child and ask: Who is in the book? What are they doing in the pictures? Can you tell where they are (zoo, park, hospital, school, home) in the book? When your child is able to answer these questions, try asking her to pick out a couple of books that she would like to read because the pictures look fun. When your child is able to do this, ask her to pick out two books that she would like to read because she thinks she knows what the books are about. As your child is successful, increase the number of books while decreasing your directions.

5 | Tag Reading

TIME: 20 minutes

MATERIALS
▪ storybook (see appendix A for suggestions)

Learning happens when: you and your child sit down to read together. Tell your child that you are going to take turns reading and that you are going to tag each other when it is the other's turn to read. After you read the entire story by tagging each other to read aloud, say "Now I will tell you three things about the story and you tell me which one best describes the story." Follow up with sequence questions, such as asking your child to tell you what happened first, second, and third in the story. Don't worry about whether your child skips things that happened. You are only trying to see if he gets the events that he identifies in the proper order.

Variations: Tell your child that each person has to read at least two pages in a row but no more than five. This reinforces counting and organizational skills as well as reading skills. Tell him that you can tag each other only in the middle of a sentence.

🖐 Use a hand signal to tag your child into reading. Perhaps put up two fingers for the number of pages to read.

👁 Give your child a key word to look for while reading. If he finds it in the story, he will complete the sentence and then switch readers.

👂 Set a timer while reading. When it goes off, it's time to switch readers.

Mastery occurs when: your child is able to read aloud, maintain his place in the story, and answer the questions that you ask.

You may want to help your child a little more if: he is unable to identify the place that you leave off when he is tagged. Try following the words you are reading with your finger and tagging your child only when you are at the end of a page.

6 | Every Picture Tells a Story

Learning happens when: you read a picture book story to your child. Let your child practice reading the book silently. Ask her to retell the story to you using the pictures as clues (without reading the words). After your child has retold the story to you, write four simple sentences about the story on paper using words that you know your child can read. Ask her to circle the sentence that tells the most about the story.

TIME: 20–30 minutes

MATERIALS
- picture book (see appendix A for suggestions)
- paper
- crayons or markers

✋ Discuss with your child some of the major parts of the story, then ask her to act them out for you.

👁 If your child is particularly artistic, ask her to draw pictures that retell the story.

👂 Instead of writing the four sentences, say them to your child and ask her to write them down (with your help). Then ask her to say the one that tells about the story the best.

Mastery occurs when: your child is able to retell the story in all or most of its entirety, as well as correctly identify the sentence that best describes the story.

You may want to help your child a little more if: she is unable to properly sequence the story when retelling it. Try rereading the story and asking your child sequence-based questions (What happened before this? What was the first thing that happened? Which character was introduced first?) throughout the story and afterward.

7 | Board Games

TIME: 45 minutes

MATERIALS
▪ board game that is unfamiliar to your child; try to use a game within your child's age range (as indicated on the game).

Learning happens when: you give the game to your child without telling him how to play. Give your child time to explore the game, including looking at the directions, the game pieces, and the layout of the board. After a few minutes, ask him to tell you how to play. After he has completed his instructions, you should correct his directions if needed. Play the game with your child. Talk about the importance of following the directions and rules of the game. Ask your child how it feels to play with someone who doesn't follow the rules. When you are finished playing the game, ask him to make a list of times when it is especially important to follow rules.

✋ Play an active game such as Red Light, Green Light, or Red Rover. See if your child can make up his own rules.

👁 You may choose to rewrite the directions with your child's help on a large sheet of paper with markers or crayons.

👂 Your child can retell the directions, instructing others on how to play the game. If he doesn't understand the directions well enough to retell them, ask him to listen to you or another player retell them.

Mastery occurs when: your child is able to understand most of the rules of the game by simply looking at the game pieces, reading some or all of the directions, and looking at any pictures or diagrams provided. Your child is successfully applying the concepts taught when he is able to identify the importance of rules in the game and in other situations.

You may want to help your child a little more if: he is not able to understand most of the rules of the game on his own. Try explaining the game to your child and playing it; then choose a simpler game and retry the activity.

8 Puppet Master

Learning happens when: you and your child read the story together. Talk about the characters in the story and what they are doing. Ask your child sequence-based questions (What happens first? What do you think will happen next?). When you are finished with the story, ask your child to make puppets to show the main characters in the story using the supplies you have. When the puppets are completed, ask your child to retell the story using the puppets.

TIME: 60 minutes

MATERIALS

- storybook (see appendix A for suggestions)
- small paper bags
- art supplies (crayons, markers, glue, glitter, stickers, construction or scrap paper, and rounded-edge scissors)

Variations: Ask your child to make puppets that show all of the characters in the book, not just the main characters. Ask her to retell and extend the story using the puppets.

✋ Instead of making puppets, make props for each of the characters with your child. Then help your child retell the story by acting out the scenes.

👁 After your child has made the puppets, help her write out a brief script that retells the story. Gather the family around and put on a puppet show.

👂 Grab a tape player and retell the story with your child using different voices for different characters.

Mastery occurs when: your child is able to retell most of the story using the puppets.

You may want to help your child a little more if: she is unable to retell the story in the proper sequence. Try rereading the story, letting your child tell you what will happen next based on the pictures. You should confirm your child's answers or correct her immediately upon encountering the next part of the story. Ask your child to make another prediction when you see the next picture and talk to her about what she learned from the first prediction. When you are finished rereading the story, ask your child sequencing questions (When did this happen? What happened after that? What happened first? What happened last?). Ask your child to retell the story to you with the puppet she already made. You should give her some time to make additional puppets or to make artistic modifications to the first puppet.

9 | Which Is First? Who Is Second?

Spend some time beforehand reading the book, then writing groups of sentences about the story on the paper and cutting them into sentence strips. For example, write four sentences that tell about the story in chronological order and/or write three sentences about each character.

Learning happens when: you read the story with your child. When you have finished reading, give your child the sentence strips. Ask him to put the sentences that tell the story in the order that they happened, and then ask your child to find the sentences that describe the characters. Have your child put all of the sentences that tell about one character together and put all of the sentences that tell about another character in another pile.

TIME: 30 minutes

MATERIALS
- storybook (see appendix A for suggestions)
- paper
- crayons or markers
- rounded-edge scissors

- Race the clock. Give your child a set amount of time to put the sentences in the proper order.

- Ask your child to write out a few sentences of his own and add them to the other strips to put in order.

- Ask your child to read the sentences aloud and fill in the blanks in the story while doing so.

Mastery occurs when: your child is able to properly group all of the sentences.

You may want to help your child a little more if: he struggles with properly grouping the sentences. Try rereading the story with your child and talking to him about the story as you read it. Point out the things that he will see in the sentences and ask sequencing questions. When you have finished rereading the story, try the activity again.

10 Act Out!

TIME: 45 minutes

MATERIALS
storybook (see appendix A for suggestions)
old clothes to play dress up

Learning happens when: you and your child read the book together. Talk about the book while you are reading it. Ask your child sequencing questions as well as questions about the characters. When you have finished the story, give your child some time to dress up in a costume and think about how to retell the story. When she is ready, let her act out the story for you.

Variations: Dress up with your child and let her give you a role in the story to act out.

Act out the story with your child and videotape it. Then watch it together.

Write out a script with your child to retell the story.

Take a picture walk through the book—look at each picture in order and use the pictures as clues to retell the story.

Mastery occurs when: your child is able to act out the story without leaving big chunks out.

You may want to help your child a little more if: she is unable to act out the story to you in the proper sequence or leaves parts of the story out. Try rereading the story with her. When you are finished rereading the story, ask your child sequencing questions (When did this happen? What happened after that? What happened first? What happened last?). Ask your child to act out the story again.

Environmental Learning

There are many opportunities to reinforce or introduce early reading skills throughout the day. *Stop* should be one of the first words your child reads if your town has any street signs at all. *Mc* will be one of the first consonant blends he or she pronounces if you ever succumb to the golden arches. What is the name of your town and how many signs with the town's name do you pass each day? What is the name of your child's school and how many times do you see it printed each day?

Sequencing, or understanding that events in real life and in stories happen in a certain order, is easily taught through events in daily life. Talk with your child often about what he or she did that day or what you're planning to do that weekend.

In addition to reading signs, reading books should be a part of your daily schedule with your child. Not only do you need to read to your child but he or she needs to see that you read every day. Practicing what you preach will truly benefit your child's reading habits.

End of First Grade Reading Checklist

Students who are working at the standard level at the end of first grade:

____ Develop appropriate active strategies, such as interpreting illustrations, to construct meaning from print

____ Decode unfamiliar words

____ Understand how speech sounds are connected

____ Understand or are able to figure out (using contextual clues) the meaning of what they read

____ Develop and maintain motivation to read

____ Extend a story

____ Predict what will happen next

____ Discuss the character's motives

____ Question the author's meaning

____ Describe causes and effects of events in the text

____ Discuss books by tying their comments directly to the text

First Grade Writing 6

It is easy to think, "Okay, I taught/helped teach my child to read, whew—I'm glad that is over." But writing might be the hardest thing your child does all day. By combining reading skills with small motor skills and adding in spelling, your child is just learning to communicate via the written word—a skill that will be used and refined for the rest of your child's life.

When a first grader writes, he or she must simultaneously recall ideas, vocabulary, and rules of spelling, punctuation, and grammar while putting thoughts on paper. This can be overwhelming for children. They are trying to use a range of abilities from the higher-order problem-solving processes of brainstorming and creating ideas to the more basic movements of getting their fingers to form letters using a pencil or typing on a keyboard.

Don't despair. It is fairly common for children who possess smart, creative, thoughtful ideas to initially have a lot of trouble conveying information in writing. This chapter is intended to end some of the mystery of how all these skills come together. It will help you support your child as he or she develops writing skills.

> ## Beginning of First Grade Writing Checklist
>
> Students who are working at the standard level at the beginning of first grade:
>
> ____ Name and label objects
>
> ____ Gather, collect, and share information
>
> ____ Stay on topic (maintain focus)
>
> ____ Can write in chronological order
>
> ____ Incorporate storybook language (for example, "They lived happily ever after") into their writing
>
> ____ Think in a more extended fashion than they can write, so some thoughts must be extended orally

Handwriting

Now that your child is recognizing letters and words, it is time to take the next step for writing: actually forming the letters and words on paper. When your child writes and forms letters, he uses the coordination and control of the muscles at the end of his fingers. Some muscles are used to make a pencil move up and down, others to make the pencil move left and right, and still others to move it in a circular motion. Since writing letters requires a combination of these movements, different muscles are used to form different letters. Some children have trouble getting their muscles to move in the correct way when they write.

To learn to write letters, your child has to identify the letter to be written, use memory to recall what that letter should look like, then make and hold a mental picture of the letter while he sends signals from his brain to the finger muscles required to move the pencil and form the desired letter. Finally, your child forms the letter in the right place on the paper. That is a lot harder than you remember, isn't it?

There are several ways to introduce and reinforce writing letters that take some of the pressure off your child. For example, draw the letters with a stick in a sandbox. The motor skills required to do this are not as refined as those needed to write with a pencil. Form the letters with string, clay, or dough. Draw letters with your fingers in the air. Get large sheets of paper and crayons and write big letters.

Writing sentences and paragraphs requires your child to remember several things simultaneously (forming letters and words, using correct grammar and punctuation, recalling the ideas he wants to write). If a child has a hard time retrieving any of this information from long- or short-term memory, the entire writing process will be more difficult.

The following table describes some important skills related to handwriting, where children can run into problems, and how you can help them along.

Handwriting Skills	Having Problems?	Quick Tips
Copies easily from the board or overhead projector.	Has difficulty copying from the board or overhead projector.	Ask your child to trace and then copy from a piece of paper placed on the desk in front of him.
Writes legibly and consistently forms letters.	Writing is not legible and letter formation is inconsistent.	Employ alternate writing strategies, such as tracing.
Writes letters quickly and easily.	Has difficulty writing letters quickly and easily.	Write, write, write! This is truly a case where practice makes perfect.
Holds a pen or pencil comfortably.	Has an awkward or uncomfortable grip.	What may be awkward or uncomfortable for you may not be for your child. If your child persists in holding a pencil a certain way, it may be wise to allow it.
Easily types on a computer.	Has difficulty learning how to type on the computer.	Problems may be letter or sound association, letter combinations, or sound blending. Check out these areas.

Now that you have an idea of the mechanics of handwriting and what to expect, let's look as some activities that you can do with your child to enhance these skills.

Handwriting Activities

1 Word Shapes

Have you ever noticed that if you outline familiar words, the shape of the outline looks familiar too? You will need to make a list of words that are familiar to your child. Use lowercase letters. Create another list next to the list of words of just the outlines of the words but in an order different from the list of words.

Time: 30 minutes

MATERIALS
- graph paper
- markers
- alphabet chart

Learning happens when: you explain to your child that individual letters make up words, but the word itself actually has a shape (design). Ask your child to match the word to its shape by drawing a line. Then he should write the letters that make the design inside the shape. Graph paper is the easiest paper to begin writing words on—there is a box that guides how big the letters should be, and when you write in the box beside it, the line across the paper stands out more than the boxes on the paper. Check and correct as needed. After the matching is finished, ask your child to spell the words as you say them. You can add these words to the list for a "word wall"—a place on a wall where you and your child can post lists and other groups of words for frequent reference and discussion.

- Make letters out of clay. Your child can manipulate the clay and then form words to see what the overall shape looks like.

- Try cutting out the shapes of the words and having your child match them like puzzle pieces.

- Add a voice to the entire activity: either you, your child, or both of you say (in an exaggerated way) all of the sounds in the word you are tracing and cutting out.

Mastery occurs when: your child can visually match the shape of the word to the word, tell you the name of the letters in the word, and print the word correctly.

You may want to help your child a little more if: he has problems matching the shapes to the words. Ask him to match the word you say to the words on the graph paper and then copy them. If this is difficult, ask your child to trace the word after you write it.

2 Word Toss

Learning happens when: you explain to your child that she should toss the cube, look at the letter that it lands on, and then print as many words as she can that start with the letter until the timer sounds. You will both count the number of words. Try the activity again using the same period of time. Compare the totals to see if your child can beat her own record.

Variations: Let your child write the same letter that shows on the cube. Change the cubes often to make it more challenging, or use the same directions, but write words that end with the sound of the letter on the cube.

🖐 Get a foam brick and use a permanent marker to write the letters on it. Take the game outside and let your child use chalk and the sidewalk to write out the words.

👁 Use poster paper and colorful markers to make a sheet for each consonant. Ask your child to write words that start with each letter on the paper, count up the words, and then ask her to illustrate the words.

👂 Instead of writing the words, ask your child to say them aloud to you. When playing this way, repetition is key. Don't change the block's letters until your child has gone through each letter at least three times.

Mastery occurs when: your child forms letters correctly, writes words using the correct first letter, and beats her own time in the game.

You may want to help your child a little more if: she is unable to think of and print enough words for each letter on her own. Try

---

TIME: 15 minutes

MATERIALS

- consonant cube (you can make your own by covering a large die or something in a cube shape with paper and labeling it with various consonants)
- paper
- markers
- timer

brainstorming words with your child each time she rolls the cube but without writing them down. Progress to letting your child write the words you both brainstorm—still without the timer. When she successfully completes this portion of the activity, turn the timer on and brainstorm without writing the words down, then move to the full activity.

3 Sidewalk Chalk

TIME: 40 minutes

MATERIALS
sidewalk chalk

Learning happens when: you give your child sidewalk chalk and allow free time for drawing. Talk with your child about what he is drawing. "What is it? That starts with a what?" Let him write the words on the sidewalk. Talk to your child about what you see in the neighborhood. Write down all of the things you can see. You can help your child with spelling if you like, but it isn't necessary for each word to be spelled perfectly.

Variations: Try the activity using both capital and lowercase letters.

✋ Keep him drawing. Let your child draw or color the whole time. The movement reinforces learning.

👁 Pick a letter and ask your child to find all the things around that start with that letter and draw them on the sidewalk.

👂 Ask your child to draw pictures of things that rhyme and then to say the rhyming words to you. Write the rhyming sounds—the parts of the words that sound alike—on the sidewalk.

Mastery occurs when: your child forms the letters correctly and matches letters to the sounds that go with what he is drawing.

You may want to help your child a little more if: he forms letters incorrectly (such as backward) or has trouble matching them to the correct sounds. Try putting an alphabet chart (a list of the alphabet) on the ground for your child to look at. If this doesn't help, make dotted outlines of the letters in one color of chalk and let your child trace over them with another color.

4 | See It! Hear It! Write It!

Cut out familiar pictures that can be named with three-letter words. Glue each picture to a piece of construction paper and fold the paper into thirds. Under the picture, draw a space for each letter of the word, one space per fold.

Learning happens when: you show the pictures to your child one at a time, saying the word slowly as you draw out each consonant and vowel sound. Tell your child that she should write one letter in each of the three spaces in order to spell the word that describes the picture.

Variations: Increase the number of folds in the paper and choose pictures of things that are spelled with more than three letters.

TIME: 40 minutes

MATERIALS
- catalogs, magazines, newspaper fliers
- rounded-edge scissors
- nontoxic glue
- construction paper (cut into 4 × 6-inch pieces)

- If you have alphabet magnets on the refrigerator, put the pictures on larger pieces of paper. Instead of having your child write out each letter, ask her to walk to the refrigerator, get the first letter, and put it under the picture, then the second, then the third.

- Spell out the letters of the word for your child. Ask her to write the word on a piece of paper. Then ask her to sound out the word and illustrate the word on the paper.

- Before your child writes each letter, ask her to repeat the letter and the sound it makes within the word.

Mastery occurs when: your child forms the letters and spells the words correctly.

You may want to help your child a little more if: she is unable to write the words on her own. Try writing the words using dotted outlines, and ask your child to first trace, then write, the words.

5 | Grab Bag Letters

TIME: 30 minutes

MATERIALS
- small sheets of paper with a letter written on each one
- markers
- gift bag
- timer
- lined paper

Learning happens when: you explain that to play this game your child will try to beat his own time. He will take a letter from the bag, say the sound that it makes, then write it on the lined paper. Emphasize good handwriting. See how many letters your child can do before the timer goes off (set it at varying times, from one minute to three or four minutes). Repeat several times.

Variations: Write words instead of letters.

✋ Put the bag across the room. Ask your child to get a letter from the bag, walk back to you, and then start writing.

👁 Give your child twenty-six sheets of paper and ask him to draw simple pictures of things that start with each letter of the alphabet in addition to the letters. Use those in the bag instead of just the letters.

👂 Add a little math to this activity. Instead of using a timer, count by twos (2, 4, 6, etc.) or fives (5, 10, 15, etc.). Then switch the roles and let your child try counting for you.

Mastery occurs when: the letters are formed correctly and your child improves on his own time.

You may want to help your child a little more if: he is unable to form the letters correctly. You can help your child by writing the letters several times in a row with dotted outlines before he draws a letter. Limit the letters in the grab bag to the ones you have outlined, then let your child draw and trace the letters.

6 | Rhyme and Write

TIME: 20 minutes

MATERIALS
- rhyming book (such as one by Dr. Seuss)
- large sheet of paper
- markers
- lined paper
- pencils

Learning happens when: you read a rhyming book to your child and talk about rhymes. Tell your child that rhymes are words that sound alike at the end but have different beginning sounds. Read a few of the lines, pointing out the rhyming words to your child. Write two phrases that end with rhyming words on the large sheet of paper, but leave blanks where these words should go. Ask your child to fill in the word that rhymes on the big paper and to write the phrases that are on the big paper on the lined paper.

Variations: Use a favorite rhyming song with this activity. Continue the activity with words that are more difficult to spell.

- Clap with the rhythm of the story, especially if you're using a Dr. Seuss book. The rhythmic pattern can help your child figure out what word will fit next. Ask your child to clap the rhythm when figuring out what words to write.

- Say a word and then sound out the word as you spell it on a large piece of paper. Ask your child to write a word that rhymes with your word. Let her read the two rhyming words aloud. Continue until she is writing rhymes easily.

- Prepare a list of words that are easy to rhyme. Say a word. Ask your child to write three words that rhyme with it.

Mastery occurs when: your child can correctly match the letters to the sounds and spell the rhyming words.

You may want to help your child a little more if: she is unable to match the letters to the sounds and spell the rhyming words. Try just spelling the ending that rhymes and then writing the beginning sounds in different colors.

7 Blends

TIME: 15 minutes

MATERIALS

- paper
- markers
- list of word pairs on paper (make sure there is room to write beside the words or under them; the word pairs can be in varied formats—for example, words that begin with the same blend, such as bl or br)

Learning happens when: you give your child the list of word pairs and read a word in one of the pairs. Your child will circle the word that you say, tell you the beginning blend, then write the blend. The other word serves as a distraction. Correct as needed. Review by asking your child to say the sound that matches each blend.

✋ If you have magnetic letters, instead of giving your child a list of words, say the words and ask him to pick the letters that make up the blend from the magnetic alphabet letters.

👁 Pick words that your child can illustrate.

👂 Ask your child to say the sound that the blend makes back to you as he is writing it. Make sure to practice a lot with him.

Mastery occurs when: your child chooses the correct word when you say it and forms the letters correctly as he writes the blend.

You may want to help your child a little more if: he is unable to choose the correct word or forms the letters of the blend incorrectly. You may want to draw a dotted outline of the words for your child to trace. Retry the word pair activity but without blends; for example, use words that go together, such as "open" and "close." Overenunciate the beginning sounds. When your child masters this activity, move back to blends.

8 | Tactile Alphabet

Learning happens when: you ask your child to print the capital letters of the alphabet on the pieces of paper using markers. Instruct your child to trace each letter in glue, lay the letter in the cake pan, and then sprinkle cornmeal over the glue. Gently pick up the letter and put it aside to dry. Continue with other letters. You can use these artsy letters to make personal alphabet books or to decorate the wall in your child's room.

Variations: Instead of cornmeal, use salt, colored craft sand, glitter, or sequins.

✋ Make some colored rice or pasta with your child. You can color uncooked rice or pasta easily by pouring some into a quart- or gallon-sized plastic bag, then adding a couple of drops of food coloring and a teaspoon of alcohol. Shake the bag until the color is evenly distributed, pour the colored rice or pasta onto layers of newspaper, and let it air dry. Your child may want to try to eat the colored pasta or rice. You can fight this battle, or you can give your child a piece to eat and be done with it. It is a rare child who finishes the first piece, much less wants a second. Glue the colored rice or pasta to the letter shapes.

👁 Try using glow-in-the-dark glue to attach the decorations to each letter so that your child can see her letters even at night.

👂 Try using bubble wrap to make the letters. Your child will be able to practice tracing the movement of the letters and hear that satisfying popping noise at the same time.

Mastery occurs when: your child consistently identifies and writes the letters correctly.

TIME: 30 minutes

MATERIALS
- construction paper cut into 4 × 6-inch pieces
- markers
- nontoxic glue
- rectangular cake pan
- shaker of cornmeal

You may want to help your child a little more if: she is unable to write the letters. You may want to draw dotted outlines of the letters for her to trace.

9 Shaving Words

TIME: 30 minutes

MATERIALS
can of shaving cream
countertop or plastic placemat
dish towel or damp sponge

Learning happens when: you spray shaving cream on a clean countertop or placemat and allow your child to play in it. Explain to your child that you will say some familiar (three- to four-letter) words and that you want him to listen for three sounds—the first sound is the beginning letter, the second sound is the middle letters, and the third sound is the ending letter. Ask your child to listen carefully as you say the word and then write the word with his finger in the shaving cream. Do the first one with your child to show him what you expect. Correct spelling as needed. Also check for the correct formation of letters. Mistakes disappear with a swipe of the hand.

Variations: Introduce each sound in a separate lesson. Try spelling names of family members, using capitalization properly, or introducing blends.

Grab some paper, put on rubber gloves, and use glue and glitter instead of the shaving cream. Let your child form the letters with the glue on paper, then sprinkle the glitter on them. Watch how much glue he is using—the letters will dry much faster if they are thin, not fat. Now your child's work can be permanent and pretty.

Pick a theme from which to choose your words according to the interests of your child. Move on to word families (for example, bat, sat, cat, fat, rat).

👂 Try this activity with a simple story. While your child is manipulating the shaving cream, read the story aloud (preferably one with rhyming words or word families). At the end of each line, ask your child to write the last word.

Mastery occurs when: your child correctly forms letters of the alphabet, correctly associates the letters and their sounds, and correctly spells the words.

You may want to help your child a little more if: he is unable to write whole words or form letters correctly. Try stepping back and concentrating on beginning or ending sounds and writing one letter at a time.

10 Rolling Race

Draw lines on the piece of paper to make six rows and six columns. Make some copies of this grid either by hand or on a copy machine. Put each of the consonants on the cube in one of the six columns in the top row (this is the model for writing the letter).

Learning takes place when: you demonstrate to your child how to play the game: roll the die, say the letter, find that letter on the graph, and write it once in the proper column. Repeat until your child has used up all of the spaces in the column for one letter on the grid paper. This letter is the winner. Repeat with a fresh sheet of grid paper.

Variations: Change the letters on the cube or use more than one cube and more than one piece of paper.

TIME: 45 minutes

MATERIALS
- markers
- paper
- consonant cube (you can make your own by relabeling a large die or other cube shape, or use a sugar cube and a permanent marker)

✋ Try this activity outside with chalk and the sidewalk. Make the chart on the sidewalk and let your child fill it in based on the roll of the dice.

👁 Ask your child for help making the grid paper and the letter cube. You may want to start the cube with letters from her name.

👂 In addition to saying the letter, ask your child to say the sound it makes and a word that starts with it.

Mastery occurs when: your child consistently forms the letters correctly.

You may want to help your child a little more if: she has trouble filling in the letters. You may want to draw dotted outlines of the letters in most of the rows, letting your child trace instead of write in these rows.

11 Memory

TIME: 30–40 minutes

MATERIALS
▪ memory game (where you pair matching pictures)
▪ graph paper
▪ markers

Memory is a game where the object is to find a pair of pictures that match from cards that are lying face down. When you turn a card over to see if it matches another card you turn over, you must replace it in the same spot if there is no match. Memory is important for remembering which face-down card has which picture.

Learning happens when: you play the game according to the directions, but whenever your child gets a match, he must write the letter that makes the beginning sound of the matching pictures word on the graph paper. You may want to use homemade graph paper that has larger squares. The one who finds the most pairs with the beginning sound written correctly wins.

Variations: Do this activity, but use the ending sounds of the words instead of the beginning sounds.

✍ Play the game as you regularly would, but let your child use a stamp pad and letters to stamp the letters in the graph.

👁 Ask your child to circle or put an X over the letters that you have already written into the graph.

👂 Ask your child to say the sounds of the letters that he is putting on the graph.

Mastery occurs when: your child makes the letters that match the paired pictures correctly.

You may want to help your child a little more if: he has trouble writing the correct beginning sounds. You may want to draw dotted outlines of most of the letters, letting him trace instead of write them.

Rules of Writing

Wow, handwriting is tough. There are a lot of rules of writing, including some that are hard for even grown-ups to remember. There are punctuation and grammar rules. When they are combined with the actual mechanics of writing, your little author has a lot to remember. There are many things you can do to help your child. Let's start with the basics.

There can be an enormous difference between language use at home and at school. Using proper grammar at home, just as it is emphasized within the classroom, will provide your child with the consistent opportunity to use grammar rules properly. You don't have to sound like Shakespeare, but do try to speak in complete sentences, use proper grammar, and limit your slang. If you encourage proper speaking all of the time, you will be helping your child build and refine thinking and communication skills.

Some children may have an easy time remembering rules for mechanics and grammar when they're tackling a work sheet, but they struggle to remember everything at once while writing a sentence or a paragraph. Work on phrases first, then sentences. This isn't an unusual problem, and with some practice you will help your child overcome it.

How do you correct your child's speech or written work without being a bad guy? It is easy with speech because you can do it just by saying the correct word in a nice tone of voice. If you are looking at written work, it is tempting to get out a red pen and mark away. Don't. You have a first grader here and the most important thing you can do is give positive feedback. Accept the work as good just because your child tried, then start a conversation about what you are questioning on the paper: What does this word mean? Why did you use a capital letter here? Should a period go here? Ask your child to make a final copy that incorporates the things you talk about and change together.

To spell words correctly, kids need to have a good understanding about the sounds that make up words and how these sounds can be put together to create letters and words on paper. But they also need a good memory. Some children are very good at remembering what words look like; others may sound out words as they are spelling them. As your child progresses through school, it is very helpful if she can remember how to spell many words automatically. The more able your child is to spell a word without stopping to think about it, the more she is able to pay attention to remembering and organizing the ideas she wants to write instead of worrying about spelling.

First grade writing is an introduction to the concept that there are rules that we follow so that our writing makes sense to others.

The table on page 89 describes some important skills related to the mechanics of written language, where children can run into problems, and how you can help them along.

If your child is still writing in letter strings or relying heavily on pictures and single-word labels at the middle and end of first grade, he will particularly benefit from some extra practice on the following activities.

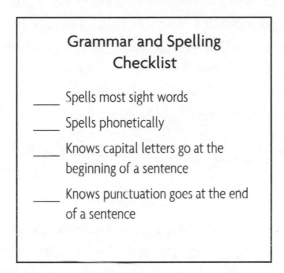

Grammar and Spelling Checklist

____ Spells most sight words

____ Spells phonetically

____ Knows capital letters go at the beginning of a sentence

____ Knows punctuation goes at the end of a sentence

Rules of Writing Skills	Having Problems?	Quick Tips
Uses correct capitalization.	Can't remember and/or use the rules for capitalization.	Read with your child while following words and sentences with your finger. Talk about how you know when a sentence is starting (capital letters).
Uses punctuation.	Can't remember and/or use the rules for punctuation.	Read with your child while following words and sentences with your finger. Talk about how you know when to take a breath when reading (the sentence ends or there is a comma).
Correctly spells most words when writing.	Frequently misspells words while writing.	Flash those flash cards. Spelling is highly dependent on memory, and the best way to aid in memorization is frequent exposure to what you need to remember.

Rules of Writing Activities

1 Journal Entry

TIME: 30 minutes

MATERIALS
- storybook about a pet
- paper
- crayons or markers
- pencils

Learning happens when: you read a story with your child about a pet. Talk about what the main character likes about his or her pet, then ask your child to draw a picture of a pet that he either has or would like to own. Ask your child to write sentences telling what he likes about that animal, and have him read the sentences aloud to you and other family members.

Variations: Look up information about an animal that interests your child. Ask him to write sentences including facts about that animal.

Go to a zoo and take a look at the animals. Help your child read the signs that accompany each animal. When you get home, ask him to write a few sentences about which animal he liked best and why.

Have your child draw an imaginary animal, then write about that animal's behavior.

Ask your child to tell you about a pet or an animal with which he is familiar. Make notes by jotting down one or two words that your child says about the animal. Ask your child to write one sentence for each of the notes you made, then read the sentences to you.

Mastery occurs when: your child forms the letters correctly, begins a sentence with a capital letter, and uses proper punctuation at the end of a sentence.

You may want to help your child a little more if: he is unable to write complete sentences on his own. Try starting with phrases and work up to sentences.

2 Apostrophe What?

Make a chart of contractions in the following way:

she	is	she's
he	is	he's
we	are	we're
was	not	wasn't
is	not	isn't

TIME: 25 minutes

MATERIALS
- large sheet of paper
- markers or pencils
- storybook, magazine, or newspaper
- lined paper

Learning happens when: you show your child the chart and spend some time talking with her about contractions and how to recognize them. Point to the two words and the contractions that represent them on the chart. Talk about apostrophes and their placement, and have your child practice making apostrophes. Ask her to look through a storybook and write every contraction she finds. Have your child use the chart you made to match the contraction to the two words that make up the contraction, then write the two matching words next to the contraction.

Variations: Do these activities, but also ask your child to use each contraction in a sentence.

- Add punctuation cards to the set of letter cards that you probably have left over from the First Grade Reading chapter and ask your child to spell the contraction out using the letter and punctuation cards.

- Have your child look through a magazine or newspaper article instead of a storybook.

- After doing this activity, practice verbally with your child by giving her the contraction and asking for the words it represents. Let your child use the chart until she is more confident.

Mastery occurs when: your child makes apostrophes correctly, matches contractions to the words they represent, and writes contractions correctly.

You may want to help your child a little more if: she is unable to properly combine the words or is unable to put the apostrophe in the proper place. Make some flash cards to reinforce the skills.

3 Using Capital Letters

TIME: 20 minutes

MATERIALS
- family photographs
- self-adhesive notes
- paper
- markers or pencils
- magnets or tape

Learning happens when: you talk with your child about using capital letters at the beginning of a sentence, with abbreviations, and with words that are names (proper nouns). Look through family photographs with your child and ask him to name the people. Use self-adhesive notes to label the photographs with the written names. Put some of the photos on your refrigerator or a bulletin board where your child can see them easily. Ask him to write sentences describing what was happening the day the photos were taken. Remind him to use capitalization, punctuation, and his best handwriting.

Variations: Ask your child to write a question about the photograph or to write cartoonlike captions. Or have him label pictures of places, book characters, classmates, teachers, and so forth.

✋ Take an instant or digital camera with you on a walk around the neighborhood. Ask your child to take pictures of things that start with a capital letter. Street signs, road signs, and store names are easy ones to find. When you get home, make a collage of things he found that start with a capital letter.

👁 The family photos can be used for writing all sorts of things, such as experience stories, invitations to places in the photos, thank-you notes for something related to the picture, and make-believe stories.

🎧 Say two words to your child—one that starts with a capital and one that doesn't, such as "California" and "bat." Ask him to pick out the word that starts with a capital.

Mastery occurs when: your child writes names using capital letters correctly and forms letters properly.

You may want to help your child a little more if: he has trouble placing the capital letter at the beginning of a name. You can start by writing your child's name and your name—names that your child is used to seeing written properly—then move on to names your child doesn't recognize as easily. If he is having trouble forming the capital letters, you may want to draw dotted outlines of the letters for him to trace. You can also draw dotted outlines of part of the letter so that your child writes the rest of the letter on his own.

4 | Ownership

Learning happens when: you ask your child to write a list of objects found around the house while you write a list of family names. Talk with your child about possessives, how to recognize them, and where to place apostrophes when writing them. You may want to make a chart similar to the contraction chart. Show your child a list of names of all family members. Review the rules about writing a name (capital letter, proper noun). Ask her to read the list of objects to you. As she reads each item from the list, ask whose it is. Demonstrate the correct way to write a possessive.

Variations: Using the list of objects, ask your child to write the name as a possessive of who owns each item. Allow her to use your list of family members for spelling help if needed.

TIME: 25 minutes

MATERIALS
- paper
- markers or pencils
- list of family names

✋ Ask your child to find objects around the house that belong to different people in the family instead of just writing a list.

👁 Gather objects from around the house that belong to various family members. Discuss possessives with your child. Then hold up an item and ask your child to write down who owns it. Ask her to create a sentence using the item and the possessive.

👂 Discuss possessives with your child. Ask her to tell you about things that belong to her, then to create a sentence using the item and the possessive. She should describe how to write the possessive as you write the sentence. After a few sentences, ask your child to write the sentences as she describes how to write possessives.

Mastery occurs when: your child can write possessives correctly and consistently. She should be able to match objects to owners and explain the apostrophe *s* added to a name. She should be able to form letters correctly and should show improvement in letter placement and spacing.

You may want to help your child a little more if: she is having trouble grasping the concept of possessives. Try making a list of the possessives opposite the list of objects, and have your child draw a line between the names and the objects that belong to them before retrying the activity.

5 Sentences

TIME: 30 minutes

MATERIALS
■ list of sentences
■ pencils

Copy the following list of sentences on a piece of paper. Leave a space below each sentence for your child to rewrite the sentence correctly:

1. please get me a dog

1. *Please give me a dog.*
   (Write this first as an example to demonstrate what to do.)

2. does she have a dog

3. i want a pet

4. will you take care of the dog

5. i will take care of it

6. can I have him now

7. what a great pet he is

8. i always wanted a dog

9. his name is max

10. max is a good dog

11. i love my dog

12. he is a great dog

Learning happens when: you talk with your child about commands, or telling sentences; questions, or asking sentences; and exclamations, or sentences that show strong feeling. Demonstrate the punctuation and voice inflections to be used with each. Write sentences such as:

1. i want a dog

2. will you get me a dog

3. wow, I'm getting a dog

Ask your child to read these sentences aloud, then read them with expression and write the proper punctuation at the end:

1. I want a dog.

2. Will you get me a dog?

3. Wow, I'm getting a dog!

Talk with your child about any mistakes. Now give him the paper that has the list of sentences on it and tell him to write them properly in the space below each sentence. Remind your child about capitalization rules and neat handwriting. It is also helpful to have him read the sentences aloud as he is writing them as a way to check his work. Ask your child to read the sentence and tell you what changes he made. Do the sentences sound different from when you read them without the changes?

Variations: Ask your child to tell you about getting a pet, or about a trip to the library or zoo. Write what he says in short sentences without capitalization or punctuation and try the activity again. Then try it again with punctuation.

Write a sentence without punctuation. Choose one that has feeling, such as "We won the game!" Ask your child to act out the sentence. Can it be done without the emotion that punctuation provides? Talk about that, and then add the punctuation that belongs to the sentence.

Look at a magazine with your child. Find a picture and ask him to tell you some things that are happening in the picture. Write them down with no punctuation and repeat the activity.

Write out a few sentences without punctuation with your child. Read the sentences aloud to him without feeling, since there is no punctuation. Then ask him to help you figure out what kind of punctuation the sentence needs and how to read it properly.

Mastery occurs when: your child writes sentences using rules of punctuation and capitalization consistently.

You may want to help your child a little more if: he is missing punctuation nuances. Try reading each sentence aloud with different punctuation. Talk about how to recognize which punctuation sounds right.

6 Capital Clock

You will want to make two sets of alphabet cards: one with capital letters and another with lowercase letters.

Learning happens when: you explain to your child that she will turn over a card that has a capital letter on it and should write the matching lowercase letter beside it. See how many cards your child can do before the timer sounds. Repeat the activity with the cards that have lowercase letters on them.

TIME: 15 minutes

MATERIALS
- index cards (for two sets of alphabet cards)
- markers or pencils
- timer

- Play Go Fish with the cards. Try to get lowercase and capital letters for a match.

- Turn it into a memory game matching capital letters to the appropriate lowercase letters.

- Turn it into a memory game matching capital letters to the appropriate lowercase letters. Ask your child to say each letter and the sounds it makes every time she turns over a card.

Mastery occurs when: your child recognizes and writes both uppercase and lowercase letters.

You may want to help your child a little more if: she is unable to identify or write the lowercase or capital letters. Try letting her look at an alphabet chart the first couple of times you do this activity.

7 Long E

TIME: 30 minutes

MATERIALS
- paper
- pencils
- word lists

Learning happens when: you tell your child that he will learn to write words that have the long *e* sound. Tell him that the sound can be spelled ee, as in see; ie, as in field; and ea, as in leaf. Remind him that when two vowels appear together they make only one sound.

You are going to read words from a list that your child should segment (pick out the beginning, middle, and ending sounds), spell, and write. Fold the paper into thirds, forming three columns. Ask your child to write the word "see" in one column. As you read out the words he should write the others that are spelled with ee in the same column. When you've finished with ee words, switch to ie words in the second column and ea words in the third column. Remind your child that the words in each column will sound alike—they will all have either ee, ie, or ea in them. Have him try writing sentences using each word. Remind him to use punctuation and capitalization as he writes.

Use these word lists:

ee: see, need, keep, green, peel, reel

ie: field, thief, chief, yield, grief

ea: leaf, bean, lead, treat, peak, seal

Variations: Try this activity with *a*, *i*, *o*, and *u*.

✋ Read a book with your child and ask him to pick out the words with the long *e* sound on each page. Ask him to choose the alphabet cards that make up that long *e* sound (without looking at the book).

👁 Ask your child to read a short story with you. Then go back through the story and ask him to write down words with the long *e* sound.

👂 Read a book with your child and ask him to pick out the words with the long *e* sound on each page. Ask your child to read the long *e* words aloud, then to spell them aloud without looking at the book.

Mastery occurs when: your child realizes the different ways to spell the long *e* sound and spells it correctly in common words. He should form letters correctly and show improvement in letter placement and spacing. He should write sentences using the rules of capitalization and punctuation.

You may want to help your child a little more if: he has trouble spelling the long *e* sound or does not seem to progress in the placement of letters, their spacing on the paper, or in writing complete sentences. Try this activity with one-syllable words with short vowel sounds. Also try writing shorter sentences, using larger sheets of paper, and writing in colors.

8 | Prefixes

TIME: 20 minutes

MATERIALS
- small sheets of paper
- word list (your list can be from school or words that your child had trouble with in other activities; if you don't have a list of words that contain prefixes, you can find one that is appropriate for your child at www.knowledgeessentials.com)
- pencils
- small gift bag
- lined paper

Write one word from a list of words on each small sheet of paper. Fold the papers and put them in the gift bag.

Learning happens when: you talk with your child about prefixes. Tell her that dis- and un- are prefixes that mean "the opposite of" or "not" (for example, unhappy means not happy or the opposite of happy). Tell your child to draw a slip of paper from the bag, add a prefix to the word, and write that word on the lined paper. Then have her use both words in a sentence and write it down. Remind her to use capitalization and punctuation. Continue until you have used all of the words. Ask your child to read her sentences to you, and check the handwriting, capitalization, and punctuation.

✋ Give your child a word that can have dis- or un- as a prefix, such as happy. Ask your child to act the opposite way and then to tell you the word with the dis- or un- prefix.

👁 Ask your child to illustrate the original word and the new word with the prefix.

👂 Before writing this activity out, do it orally.

Mastery occurs when: your child understands the meaning of words with prefixes added, uses good handwriting, and writes complete sentences using the rules of capitalization and punctuation.

You may want to help your child a little more if: she has trouble understanding prefixes or does not seem to progress in letter placement and spacing or in writing complete sentences.

9 Vowel Tree

TIME: 20 minutes

MATERIALS
- poster board
- nontoxic paints
- paintbrush
- colored paper
- rounded-edge scissors
- crayons or markers
- timer
- nontoxic glue or tape

Paint a tree trunk and bare branches on the poster board.

Learning happens when: you explain to your child that this activity uses his knowledge of long vowels (rain, stay, see, like, lake, etc.). Your child should cut out leaf shapes from colored paper. Say a long vowel word and ask your child to write as many words with the same vowel sound as possible before the timer sounds. Each word should be written on a single leaf, and your child should be encouraged to use his best handwriting. Ask him to read the words to you as you check the handwriting and spelling. All correctly written and spelled words can be glued to the tree. Continue with other long vowel sounds, adding them to the same tree.

Variations: Require same spelling of long vowel sounds for the words, such as "bite" and "kite," switch spellings, and continue. Have your child group all of the same vowel sounds around the same spot on the tree. Use words with short vowel sounds. Change colors on the tree as the seasons change, or perhaps add fruit for summer. Use the tree as a springboard for writing activities. (For example, discuss animals that live in trees. Then work with your child to research and write a report about one or more of them.)

✋ This activity is perfect by itself for your learner who likes to move.

👁 This activity is also really good without any changes for your visual learner, but you can make it even more appealing by using colored markers to write the words and making the vowel sounds different colors from the rest of the words. Ask your child to use the same color for the same vowel sounds (such as orange for long *e*, red for short *e*).

👂 As long as your auditory learner is talking or being talked to about the task at hand, the learning will likely hit home. This activity is good because there are many opportunities to talk about the activity while your child is doing it. You can also ask him to say each word aloud.

Mastery occurs when: your child can write the vowel sounds that he hears in words, form letters correctly, and spell the words correctly.

You may want to help your child a little more if: he has trouble spelling the vowel sound, does not form letters correctly, or does not progress in letter placement and spacing.

Environmental Learning

You have many opportunities to let your child practice writing by just completing your daily activities. Try letting her write the grocery list as you say what you need. (You may want to have a backup list—you know, one that you can read.) Life is full of opportunities to make lists—let your child write as many of them as possible. Ask her to write titles for her drawings or to write sentences about her art.

Reading and writing are two of the hardest subjects because they are often the basis by which we learn other subjects. Be patient with your child, but challenge her on a regular basis. Model good handwriting, language, spelling, and above all, read for information and for pleasure with and in front of your child.

End of First Grade Writing Checklist

Students who are working at the standard level at the end of first grade:

____ Communicate in writing

____ Reread their writing to monitor meaning

____ Begin to use feedback to change their writing either by adding more text or by making minor revisions

____ Revise their writing by inserting text in the middle rather than just at the end

____ Make deliberate choices about the language they use

____ Use punctuation and capitalization more often than not

First Grade Math

7

Reading and writing are important and challenging skills for your first grader to learn, but math comes in close behind them. In first grade your child is continuing work done in kindergarten to develop a formal understanding of numbers and other math concepts. Physical models play a fundamental role in helping first graders understand math concepts. If you walked in on your first grader's math lesson, you would find him or her working with physical models, or "manipulatives," of all kinds.

First grade math generally comprises sets of skills that can be divided into groups such as number sense, geometry, operations, and problem solving. *Number sense* is a set of math skills that describes your child's understanding that numbers represent quantity, and you can use numbers to count quantity, or "how many." *Geometry* concepts focus on identifying shapes. For our first grade purposes, those concepts are combined with number sense concepts. *Operations* is a set of math skills that enable your child to increase or decrease numbers by

---

Beginning of First Grade Math Checklist

Students who are working at the standard level at the beginning of first grade:

_____ Understand that numbers are symbols that tell you how many

_____ Know about time and can tell hours

_____ Recite numbers 1 through 20 corresponding to flash cards

_____ Combine and separate sets using objects

_____ Classify and sort shapes

_____ Solve addition facts through 10

_____ Compare more, less, and same

_____ Recognize half of a whole object

putting them together with symbols that tell you what to do (for first grade, this means addition, subtraction, and measurement). *Problem solving* describes using math skills to solve a problem.

Number Sense

To progress in math, your child must acquire several conceptual building blocks. These building blocks are referred to as number sense and they include:

- Numbers and counting to 100

Number Sense Skills	Having Problems?	Quick Tips
Understands mathematical symbols and can visualize patterns, math concepts, and the parts of a problem in his head.	Has difficulty visualizing patterns or the parts of a math problem in his head. Has difficulty associating math symbols with the concepts they represent.	Pattern this! Talk about patterns that you see in everyday life. Is there a pattern to be found in the cars at the stoplight (red, black, trucks, cars)? What about the lines in the sidewalk? Look for patterns in nature.
Understands math vocabulary words and is able to build math knowledge through the use of math language.	Is not comfortable using mathematical language, or has difficulty with math vocabulary words.	Try using math words in everyday situations, such as "I need bread plus milk plus apples from the grocery store. I need three things."
Understands how math concepts are related (as in the relationship between addition and subtraction, or between ratio and proportion).	Has difficulty seeing how math concepts (such as addition and subtraction, or ratio and proportion) are related to each other.	Usually the best way to a child's memory is through her stomach. Tell your child how many cookies you are going to give her. Give one less, wait for the wail, and add another.
Understands math word problems that he reads, even when irrelevant information is given, or when information is given in an order different from the order of the computation.	Is confused by the language of word problems, such as when irrelevant information is included or when information is given out of sequence.	Talk, talk, talk, math, math, math. Relate as many activities to math as possible. Use math terms and practice simple math problems as often as possible.

- The language used in math, from concepts such as measurement and money to the technical vocabulary of math, such as greater than, less than, add, subtract, difference, and sum
- An understanding of ratio and proportion
- Recognizing colors, shapes, and patterns

The table on page 104 describes important skills related to understanding number sense concepts, where children can run into problems, and how you can help them along.

Number Sense Activities

1 Shape It!

Learning happens when: you and your child shape the sugar cookie dough into triangles, circles, squares, and rectangles. Talk about the shapes as you are making them. Bake the cookies according to the package directions, then decorate with frosting and sprinkles.

Variations: You can do a lot of different activities—color each shape a specific color, make the same number of each shape, and so on.

✍ Count the cookies by twos and fives. Package the cookies in groups by shape, pattern, color, and so on, and pack them in your child's lunch box for a snack.

👁 Mix up the colors and lay the cookies out in patterns (for example, red triangle, blue circle, yellow triangle, red circle, red triangle, blue circle, yellow triangle, red circle).

👂 Follow the instructions for visual learners but read the pattern aloud: red triangle, blue circle, yellow triangle, red circle, red triangle, and so on.

TIME: 60 minutes

MATERIALS
▪ sugar cookie dough (use food coloring if you want to color the dough)
▪ cookie cutters that make geometric shapes, or a butter knife
▪ different colored frosting and sprinkles

Mastery occurs when: your child successfully identifies the correct shapes, colors, patterns, and quantities for the version of the activity that you completed.

You may want to help your child a little more if: he is unable to identify the correct shapes, colors, and quantities. Try the activity again with fewer shapes and colors.

2 | Candy Math

TIME: 15 minutes

MATERIALS
■ bag of colored candies

Learning happens when: you and your child pour some colored candies onto a clean surface. Sort all of the candies by colors. Separate three of one color and two of another color. Add 2 and 3—how many is that? Make an AB pattern (an AB pattern means that there are two things that repeat, such as red, green, red, green), then try an ABC pattern. Form a square while making the pattern. Form a circle, then a triangle. Ask your child to name each shape before eating the candies.

🖐 This activity caters to learners who need to hold and move something.

👁 Let your child look at pictures of geometric shapes and ask her to put the candies in the shape that she sees.

👂 Give your child oral instructions on what pattern or shape to make. Ask her to describe the pattern or shape.

Mastery occurs when: your child is able to represent numbers, perform simple operations, and form patterns and shapes with the candies.

You may want to help your child a little more if: she is unable to associate numbers and math terms with the candy pieces. Try the activity with groups of five or fewer candies. When your child masters the lower numbers, move on to numbers above 5.

3 | Block It to Me

TIME: 30 minutes

MATERIALS
▪ colored blocks

Learning happens when: you and your child use colored blocks to make patterns and shapes. Ask your child to count out a certain number of blocks and to build a square or a rectangle. Ask him to count out a certain number of blocks, then take some away—how many are left? Write down a number and ask your child to count out that number of blocks.

✍ Ask your child to build a block structure. Tell him to take away four blocks (or some other amount)—and not from the top. What happens? Is the structure still standing? Why? Did it fall? Why?

👁 Create a block pattern either with block sizes or colors. Ask your child to continue the pattern.

👂 Ask your child to build a block structure and then tell you about what he built. He should describe it as if he were telling an audience about a new car or a new toy.

Mastery occurs when: your child successfully completes the tasks of making patterns and shapes, counting, and addition and subtraction.

You may want to help your child a little more if: he is unable to associate the mathematical requests with the blocks. Try limiting the numbers to a range of three (such as 4, 5, and 6 only), and practice those three numbers together until your child masters them. Then move on to a new range of numbers.

4 | Fruit Roll-Up

TIME: 30–45 minutes

MATERIALS
- paper
- crayons

Take a trip to the produce section of your grocery store or visit a farmers' market.

Learning happens when: you and your child look at the colors and shapes of the fruits and vegetables. Count out four red apples and weigh them. Ask your child to find three fruits and/or vegetables that are yellow. Let her pick out one type of fruit or vegetable to take home. Count out enough so that each family member can have one. Repeat variations of these activities for ten or fifteen minutes.

✋ Give your child a small list of fruits and vegetables to find, but don't use the proper names. Use descriptions such as "It's mostly red, a little green, and round." Then see if your child can locate a tomato or an apple.

👁 When you get home, ask your child to write down how many of each fruit or vegetable you purchased. Let her draw the number of each fruit or vegetable in a row, making an easy form of a bar graph.

👂 Give your child oral directions such as "Please pick out two yellow vegetables."

Mastery occurs when: your child successfully identifies the colors, shapes, and quantities of fruits and vegetables you saw at the market.

You may want to help your child a little more if: she is unable to pick out a certain color or shape or count out an exact number. Isolate the skill with which she needs help and review the names of shapes, names of colors, or the amount that equals a number, then try this activity again.

5 Sum It Up!

Write the math terms "addition," "subtraction," and "equals" on index cards and their symbols on other index cards. Write numbers from 0 to 10 on separate index cards and the names of the numbers on other index cards.

TIME: 30 minutes

MATERIALS
- index cards
- markers

Learning happens when: you lay some of the cards out to make math sentences with words and have your child make the same sentence underneath using the cards with numbers and symbols. Then do the reverse by using the numbers and symbols to make sentences and asking your child to make the same math sentence with word cards.

- Use blocks or small items in addition to the cards. If your child is having difficulty, he can use these to help.

- Ask your child to help you create the original cards. Once he is more comfortable with this activity, let him create new math sentences to try.

- Ask your child to read the math sentences to you aloud.

Mastery occurs when: your child successfully associates the math symbols with their written names and uses them appropriately.

You may want to help your child a little more if: he is unable to pick out the symbol that matches the word or uses the words inappropriately. Focus on the symbol or words that your child is misusing, review them, then try the activity again.

6 Money Honey

TIME: 20–40 minutes

MATERIALS

▪ coins (a coin jar or several days of leftover change)

▪ coin rolls or plastic bags

▪ markers

Learning happens when: you give your child the jar of coins and talk about them with her. How would you sort them? Are they all the same size or the same color? Why are some coins the same and others different? Your child should have a basic understanding of the differences in the coins. You are reviewing denominations and sums to one dollar as well as helping your child develop the ability to identify different attributes of the coins—the shapes, weights, colors, pictures, and so on. Ask your child to sort the coins, putting each type of coin in a stack of ten.

✋ After your child has stacked all of the coins, take the coin rolls and talk about how many coins go in them. Put the coins in groups that equal one dollar. Roll them in the proper amounts or put them in plastic bags with the amount written on them.

👁 Grouping coins that look alike is right up your visual learner's alley. You may want to ask your child to record the results by writing the total number of coins and the total dollar amount of each set of coins on a bar graph.

👂 Ask your child to skip count (count by twos, fives, etc.) aloud while totaling the coins.

Mastery occurs when: your child successfully sorts the coins according to type into stacks of ten.

You may want to help your child a little more if: she is unable to sort the coins. Try limiting the coins to pennies and either nickels, dimes, or quarters. Talk about the size of the coins and the color, and try again. If your child is unable to stack the coins in tens, try having her stacking them in fives.

Operations

Mathematical operations include adding and subtracting, multiplying and dividing; they also include measuring, weighing, telling time, and completing other mathematically oriented tasks. Here are the main operations your first grader will be learning.

Math Facts

Math facts are the addition, subtraction, multiplication, and division computations, such as $2 + 2 = 4$ and $5 \times 5 = 25$, which are the basis for all math operations. First grade math facts are based on adding and subtracting single-digit numbers. It is important to get these basic skills in place before moving on to other math concepts. You want your child to be able to use them quickly and accurately when working with math procedures, learning math concepts, and performing math problem solving.

Measurement

Measuring height, weight, volume, and time begins in first grade. Your child will begin to use words such as weight, length, width, feet, inches, liter, and gallon. Calendars and clocks are used on a daily basis. First graders use formal and informal measurements. Formal measurements use a standard measuring tool, such as a ruler or measuring cup. Informal measurements are taken by measuring something without an official measuring tool, such as measuring a table in hand lengths. Your child will need to understand that measurements are math facts that can be added and subtracted.

The table on page 112 describes important skills related to learning mathematical operations, where children can run into problems, and how you can help them along.

Operations Skills	Having Problems?	Quick Tips
Shows an understanding of numbers and number values, and an awareness of the basic patterns in numbers.	Does not have a strong sense of numbers. Does not understand that there are basic patterns in numbers.	Count aloud by 2s, 5s, and 10s in daily life as much as possible.
Shows a consistent mastery of math facts up to 18.	Is inconsistent, remembering some math facts while forgetting others.	If your child understands how to add single-digit numbers and does it correctly on paper or with manipulatives, work on memorizing simple math facts such as 1 plus 1 equals 2.
Can see how math concepts (such as proportion or measurement) apply to everyday life.	Has problems transferring concepts learned in the math classroom to real-life situations.	Use addition and subtraction during snack time and playtime (with toys and time). Measure all the time—formally with measuring tools such as a ruler and informally with blocks, hands, etc.

Operations Activities

1 Growing, Growing, Gone

TIME: 5 minutes
each month

MATERIALS
- scale
- measuring tape
- paper
- crayons or markers

Learning happens when: you track your child's height (inches only and feet and inches) and weight on a regular basis (for example, the second Thursday of each month). Ask your child to fill in a chart that tracks his growth each month. Use one color for height and a different color for weight. Calculate height or weight changes (you will have to help by isolating the single-digit numbers to add or subtract, but don't do the calculation completely by yourself). Ask your child if there are other ways to tell if he has grown.

✋ Ask your child to track the weight and growth of a plant that you start from a seed.

👁 Ask your child about informal measurements: can he reach something that he couldn't reach before? Are his pant legs or sleeves too short now? Are his arms growing more quickly than his legs or are they growing at the same rate? Have your child keep track of these measurements.

👂 Ask your child to help you weigh the produce at the supermarket. Count how many things you are picking up and say the weight aloud. Have your child make predictions about how much the next thing will weigh. Put the item on the scale to see if it's heavier or lighter than what your child expected. Use that information to make the next prediction more accurate.

Mastery occurs when: your child is able to accurately weigh himself and write down the correct numbers when recording his growth.

You may want to help your child a little more if: he is unable to accurately weigh himself or is unable to write down the correct numbers when recording his growth. Isolate the specific stumbling block and go over that skill specifically with your child.

2 Kitchen Quantities

Learning happens when: you select some solids and liquids for you and your child to measure in the kitchen. Experiment by letting your child measure the same thing with several different tools, such as water with a teaspoon, a cup, and a gallon pitcher. Compare different measurements: Is a cup more than a gallon? Ask your child to say and record the measurements on a piece of paper. Look at the markings on a stick of butter or margarine. Cut a pizza or a pie in half and talk about fractions.

TIME: 20 minutes

MATERIALS
- things to measure
- measuring cups
- measuring spoons
- gallon pitcher
- paper
- pencils

✋ Get your child to help you make a small snack or meal that requires measurements.

👁 Ask your child to find out how many tablespoons there are in a cup. How about how many cups in a gallon? Ask her to write down her observations.

👂 Find the recipe for homemade play dough at www.knowledge essentials.com. Ask your child to read each ingredient and the amount needed. Then ask her what measuring tool she should use. Talk about it while you are measuring and mixing.

Mastery occurs when: your child grasps the language of measuring and the concepts associated with quantity.

You may want to help your child a little more if: she misuses the language of measuring or does not understand the concepts associated with quantity. Try the same activity with fewer measuring tools, and use only the terms "more" and "less."

3 Rock around the Clock

TIME: 20 minutes

MATERIALS
▪ analog and digital clocks
▪ paper plates (the white, thin kind)
▪ markers

Learning happens when: you set the clock to a time that is either on the hour or on the half hour. Ask your child to say what time the clock shows and then to draw a clock on the paper plate with the same time as the real clock. Use the crimped edges of the plate to divide the clock into minutes.

✋ Have your child *be* a clock. His hands are the minute hand and his legs are the hour hand. Mark out the hour on the floor with index cards and have your child emulate the hour.

👁 Ask your child to draw analog and digital clocks, and draw in the time that you say.

👂 Give your child a clock with a chime that sounds the hours and half hours. Have him give you updates at half past the hour and on the hour.

Mastery occurs when: your child correctly identifies and represents the times that you put on the clock.

You may want to help your child a little more if: he is unable to correctly identify the time. Try just asking about hours. When your child has successfully identified the hours for a few days in a row, move on to half hours.

4 | Add It Up!

Learning happens when: you say a single-digit number and tell your child to add or subtract it from another number. Have your child write down the math sentence that you just said and complete the sentence by performing the math task. Do this several times.

TIME: 10 minutes

MATERIALS

▪ paper
▪ pencils

✋ Make single-digit piles of small items, such as seven small erasers, four cherries, and one golf ball. Lay them out on the table in small baskets. When you ask your child the math sentence, have her grab the baskets that correspond to the number. That way, if your child needs to work out the problem, the items are there for her to manipulate.

👁 If your child learns better visually, ask her to draw the math sentence using tick marks, squares, or other markings to represent the numbers.

👂 Ask your child to read the math sentences back to you. If the answer is wrong, ask her to take another look at the math problem.

Mastery occurs when: your child correctly completes the operation.

You may want to help your child a little more if: she does not write the math sentence that you say aloud or incorrectly completes the operation. Try writing a few problems down and saying one of them aloud. Ask your child to circle the math sentence that you just said, read the sentence aloud to you, and complete the problem using manipulatives (anything that you have around the house to count).

5 | Clock around the Block

TIME: 10 minutes

MATERIALS
- watch with a second hand
- paper
- pencils

Learning happens when: you and your child time things, such as how many jumping jacks he can do in ten seconds, or how long it takes him to go upstairs and back down or to run to the end of the block and back. Do this activity several different ways—whatever is suitable for where you live. Talk to your child about the division of a clock and how to count by fives when looking at the clock.

👋 Try this activity with household chores. How long does it take to bring the trash to the curb? Pull weeds? Fold the laundry?

👁 Give your child the watch to time *you*. Ask your child to compare his times with yours. Ask him to subtract the times to find out the differences between them.

👂 Count aloud with your child. How many sets of five are there in your final number? How can you tell?

Mastery occurs when: your child is able to measure and record the correct times.

You may want to help your child a little more if: he is unable to measure and record the correct times. Try doing the timing and recording with your child by either timing something or someone else or by using a big clock and doing something that you can do in front of the clock, such as jumping rope or twirling. Tell your child that it is easier to time when you wait to start until the second hand reaches the 12 or the 6. Remind him how to count by fives.

Problem Solving

Your first grader is going to be asked to solve math problems, and there are essential skills—building blocks—that will allow your child to succeed. Up to this point we have been working on those building blocks.

Problem-Solving Skills	Having Problems?	Quick Tips
Estimates to help solve math problems.	Inappropriately guesses at math problems.	Estimate using halves and wholes only, then move on to numbers.
Applies previously learned math procedures to new and different situations.	Cannot transfer math procedures from learning activities to other situations.	Talk about the math involved in real life every chance you get
Determines the reasonableness of a math solution.	Accepts unreasonable math solutions.	Illustrate a few math concepts in an unreasonable fashion using things around the house. For example, talk about how many things you need to set the table while helping your child set it: Do you need 4 plates for 2 people? If you need 5 settings, does that mean that you need 8 glasses?
Can use mental imagery to conceptualize math activities and can create a picture of a math word problem in his mind.	Has difficulty using mental pictures (such as patterns or shapes) to represent math concepts, or has difficulty seeing the math problem in his mind.	Manipulate it! Use manipulatives to represent the math concepts. After your child understands the concept with manipulatives, remove part of them to get him to visualize the number you are "taking away" while seeing the part of the problem that you are "taking from" (for example, 4 apples minus 2 apples equals how many?).

Now let's start using some of them. Solving a math problem can be easy once your child has the tools to do it. Math problems are great because they have obvious rules. One plus one equals two all the time.

The table on page 117 describes important problem-solving skills, where children can run into problems, and how you can help them along.

Problem-Solving Activities

1 ABC Patterns

TIME: 15 minutes

MATERIALS
▪ a few sets of common small objects (such as game pieces, beans, dice, erasers, or paper clips)

Learning happens when: you make a pattern with objects (an ABC pattern uses three objects that alternate, an ABCD pattern uses four objects, and so on), leaving one or two objects out of the pattern. Give those objects to your child along with a couple of extra objects. Ask him to look at the pattern and to place the correct objects in the places where they are needed.

✋ Gather more people to play the pattern game. One person starts off with a motion, such as raising her right hand. The next person repeats the first person's motion and adds his own. The third person repeats the pattern and adds her motion to the pattern. Continue until someone breaks the pattern.

👁 You can also ask your child to extend the pattern. Let him rearrange the objects or add new ones to create another pattern.

👂 Are there patterns that you can hear? Yes, rhymes are patterns, poems can be patterns, and many songs have patterns. Choose a song that your child likes (with a repeating chorus) and sing it with him. Clap to the beat during the parts of the song that repeat.

Mastery occurs when: your child recognizes and extends the patterns that you make.

You may want to help your child a little more if: he is unable to recognize or extend the patterns. Try starting with a simple AB pattern (two objects that alternate) and ask your child to continue the pattern. Create another AB pattern, but this time leave missing parts and ask your child to fill them in.

2 Measuring Mystery

Learning happens when: you show your child an item and tell her that you can't figure out the best way to measure it. Give your child a choice of measuring tools. Ask her to pick out the most appropriate measuring device to help you measure the item.

TIME: 10 minutes

MATERIALS
- something to measure
- some measuring tools (ruler, measuring cup, pitcher, etc.)

👋 Let your child measure the item on her own. Don't forget about alternate forms of measurement. Give her a paper clip and ask her to find out how long a table is in paper clips. How many steps long is the hall rug?

👁 Ask your child to measure herself. Get some butcher paper and lay it out. Have your child lie down on the paper and mark where her head and feet are. Hand your child the different types of measuring tools and ask her to use whatever seems most appropriate to measure her height on the paper.

👂 Chant the equivalent measures (3 teaspoons equals 1 tablespoon, 12 inches equals 1 foot, etc.). Is there a way to make a rhyme? Work on a chant with your child and then say it a lot.

Mastery occurs when: your child chooses the proper measuring device.

You may want to help your child a little more if: she does not choose the proper measurement instrument. If you are measuring length and your child chooses a measuring cup, talk about how you would fit the item you are measuring into the cup. Could you? Can something be 1 cup long? Review the concepts of formal measurement (measurement using the proper instruments) with your child and try the activity another time with a new object to measure.

3 | Party Planning

TIME: 30–45 minutes

MATERIALS
- paper
- pencils

Learning happens when: you and your child plan a party (such as a birthday, holiday, or special dinner) together. The party can be real or imaginary. How many people will you invite? Will you serve a snack or a meal? How do you know how much to buy or how much to make? Make a list of all the things you will need together. If you have fifteen people, how many cupcakes will you need? Will you play games? How many people can play at once? What will you have to drink? Do you need a gallon or a liter or more? How many cups do you need? What will happen if more people than you plan for come to the party?

✋ Make treat bags for each guest. How many of each item do you need so that everyone gets one? Have your child sort the things into equal groups and then put the groups into the bags.

👁 Have your child draw pictures of how the room will be set up for the party. Ask him to include the food, how many people will be there, the decorations, and so forth.

🦻 Ask your child to say the directions to the games you are play-ing at the party. He should practice giving the directions a few days before the party and on the day of the party. Ask your child to greet the guests.

Mastery occurs when: your child demonstrates an ability to prob-lem solve in planning for the party to make sure that the amount of things you have is proportional to the number of people at the party.

You may want to help your child a little more if: he guesses wildly or gives unrealistic answers. Reduce the number of people expected by 1, then increase by 2. Do you double the amount of things for two people (for every one thing you had, you now need two)?

4 | Just Can't Get Enough

Learning happens when: you take your child to a local store that has lots of things she will want to buy. Let her point out some things that she would like to have. Now tell her that you are going to give her a certain amount of money. If she spends the money today, that's all the money she gets. But if she doesn't spend the money for a week, you will give her another dollar to go with it. Talk about the choice with your child. What are the benefits of spending the money now? What are the benefits of waiting? Dis-cuss the concept of a savings account with her. Let your child make her own decision.

TIME: 60 minutes

MATERIALS

▪ $5 or $10

🖐 Play "bank" and let your child start saving her money with you as the bank. At the end of the month or week, depending on how you want to do it, add in the interest. Show your child how saved money can grow on its own. When your child has enough, take her to a real bank and open a savings account.

👁 Before hitting the store, show your child circulars from two different toy stores. Ask her to compare the prices of items in which she is interested. Are they the same in both stores? What is the difference?

👂 While in the store, ask your child to read you the prices of the items she would like to have. Which items are more expensive? Which are less? If they are simple enough prices, ask your child to figure out how much more expensive one item is than another. You may want to help her round up to the nearest dollar.

Mastery occurs when: your child makes an informed decision and understands the implications of the decision.

You may want to help your child a little more if: she is unable to comprehend the implications of the choice. You may want to try repeating the activity at home by asking her to use or save privileges, such as getting to stay up fifteen minutes later tonight or thirty minutes later on the next weekend night.

5 | Orange You Hungry?

TIME: 10 minutes

MATERIALS
▪ orange

Learning happens when: you tell your child that you want to eat one-third of an orange but that you don't know how much that is. Peel the orange and take the wedges apart with your child. Can you divide the wedges into three equal piles? Are there one or two wedges left over? How can you divide the leftover wedges?

✋ Gather a few different fruits and ask your child to help you make equal amounts of fruit salad for each member of your family.

👁 Try this activity with a pizza. Ask your child to draw his findings.

👂 As you are separating the orange wedges, count out each piece aloud. Then have your child count out groups of three. Do the same activity with groups of four to explain one-quarter.

Mastery occurs when: your child is able to divide the orange into three equal parts while understanding that each part is one-third of the orange.

You may want to help your child a little more if: he is unable to conceptualize that to eat one-third of the orange you need to divide it into three equal parts. Try the activity with one-half of the orange.

6 | Dress Up

Make a list of basic clothing items with whole number prices next to them. Make sure you have a few pricing options for each type of item.

TIME: 30 minutes

MATERIALS
- paper
- pencils

Learning happens when: you and your child brainstorm a list of things a person needs to wear to be fully clothed at home (this means you don't need a jacket or other outdoor items). The basics are undergarments, socks, pants or a skirt, a shirt, and shoes. Explain to your child that you need to buy an outfit and you can only spend a certain amount of money, such as $30. You need to have all of the basic items to be fully dressed, but you want to spend the least amount of money possible. Brainstorm with her to find the best prices.

✋ Be a cashier and let your child actually collect the items and bring them to you to "buy."

👁 Use real money when doing this activity to give your child a visual representation of the purchase.

👂 Discuss different bills used to pay for items. What are all of the different combinations you can come up with to equal an amount?

Mastery occurs when: your child can use math and problem-solving skills to figure out the most appropriate clothing options.

You may want to help your child a little more if: she cannot figure out how to successfully purchase an entire outfit for the specific dollar amount. Start off smaller—instead of clothes, use food items and pick a smaller amount to spend.

Environmental Learning

You have many opportunities to reinforce basic math skills on a daily basis. A majority of the activities listed in this chapter can be completed during the course of your daily routine. Count by twos, fives, and tens in rhythm just for fun. Talk to your child about time. If you are going to play for thirty minutes, what time will it be when you stop playing? Interacting with your child in a way that reinforces math skills is easier than you think.

End of First Grade Math Checklist

Students who are working at the standard level at the end of first grade:

____ Work with patterns and sequences

____ Add and subtract single-digit numbers

____ Tell time by hours and minutes

____ Estimate and predict simple outcomes

____ Count money

____ Identify place values to hundreds

____ Practice measuring length, capacity, and weight

____ Work with geometric shapes

____ Become familiar with the concept of symmetry

____ Count higher than 100

____ Identify the fractions $\frac{1}{2}, \frac{1}{3}, \frac{1}{4}$

____ Solve simple word problems

First Grade Science

8

First grade science is a welcome opportunity for kids to do lots of hands-on exploration. Although science curricula can vary, first graders are often expected to learn about living and non-living systems, rocks and soil, and all kinds of changes, such as changes in frozen water when heat is applied, changes in the weather, and changes that happen as living things grow.

First grade science usually alternates days (or months) with social studies and almost always takes place in the afternoon. Science concepts tend to overlap with social studies concepts at this level, and the curricula tend to comprise smaller books that cover just one topic, or unit, at a time. The people who write the materials take great care to adjust the reading level so that it coincides with skill sets being learned in other areas; you won't find a two-syllable word in the first nine weeks of science materials.

Beginning of First Grade Science Checklist

Students who are working at the standard level at the beginning of first grade:

_____ Understand the difference between day and night

_____ Understand the difference between summer and winter

_____ Know the difference between most living and nonliving things

_____ Identify things necessary for sustaining life (food, water, shelter)

_____ Match mothers to babies

_____ Classify and compare animals

Systems

Systems have parts and are composed of organisms and objects that work together. First graders spend a good deal of time exploring the parts of different systems. To distinguish between a living system and a system of objects, your child will first have to tell the difference between living organisms and nonliving objects. He probably has a good start on this concept from activities in kindergarten and from general life experience. In first grade your child will refine these skills by:

- Grouping living organisms and nonliving objects
- Comparing living organisms and nonliving objects

Once your child is able to identify, compare, and contrast living and nonliving organisms and objects, it is time to look at the basic things that keep a living organism alive. Characteristics of living objects include things that allow basic needs to be met, such as leaves to soak up sun, lungs to breathe, and a mouth to eat. Your child will use that knowledge to compare and give examples of the ways living organisms depend on each other for their basic needs. He will discover that this is a living system. Many first grade teachers keep classroom pets (finches, turtles, hamsters, etc.) as a means of reinforcing concepts associated with living systems.

Learning about nonliving systems tends to be a little more kinesthetic. Your child will manipulate objects, such as toys, vehicles, or construction sets, to see how the parts work together to make a whole.

The table on page 129 describes some important concepts related to systems, where children can run into problems, and what you can do to help them along.

Living and nonliving systems give rise to numerous activities. You may want to try a few of these with your child.

Systems Concepts	Having Problems?	Quick Tips
Can easily tell the difference between living and nonliving things.	Doesn't recognize differences between living and nonliving things.	Start talking about all of the things around you in daily life that grow—living things grow—then start talking about things that aren't alive. When your child starts to identify them correctly, mix these things up and ask about both at the same time.
Understands that systems are groups of objects and/or organisms that work together.	Can't identify parts of a system.	First graders need to know that systems have parts that work together. Relate this concept to something your child is interested in, such as team sports, video games, playground equipment, and the like.

Systems Activities

1 Snacking on Plants

Learning happens when: you read the book with your child, pointing to the parts of plants as you name and define them. Talk about how all of the parts of the plants work together: the roots get nutrients and water from the soil, the leaves get food from the sun, and so on. Ask your child to point to and name the parts of plants in other books or magazines. Brainstorm a list of plant parts that we eat and let your child write the list down on paper. Choose three or four of the plant parts you can eat to make a snack. Ask your child to make a menu of the snacks by writing their names and what part of the plant they are from. (You can let him include prices and pictures on the menu, too.) Let him eat the snacks when he has completed the activity.

TIME: 45 minutes

MATERIALS
- book about plants, such as *The Carrot Seed* or *The Giant Sunflower*
- snacks that are identifiable parts of plants, such as fruit, nuts, sunflower seeds, carrots, and celery
- paper
- crayons

☝ Start a garden with your child. Try carrots or sunflowers. If you don't have enough outdoor space, try an indoor herb garden.

👁 Ask your child to make labels for the garden. Have him draw each item and write its name. Glue the labels to craft sticks and stick these in the dirt next to the place where you planted the seeds.

👂 Ask your child to say which labels should be made for the garden and then make the labels. Ask him to read them to you while you both place them in the proper spot.

Mastery occurs when: your child is able to associate the plant parts that people eat with the correct plant and name which part of a plant he is eating.

You may want to help your child a little more if: he is unable to make the connection between the plant parts that people eat and the plants that they come from.

2 It's Alive!

TIME: 15 minutes

MATERIALS
construction paper
crayons or markers

Learning happens when: you and your child talk about what makes something alive. What do living things need? Food? Water? A place to live? What do living things do? Grow? Change? What about nonliving things?

Write "It's living because" at the top of a sheet of construction paper. Talk with your child about what her favorite living thing is. It could be a plant, a pet, or a person. Ask your child to draw a picture of it under the title you wrote. After your child is done drawing, ask her to complete the sentence by writing what makes this object alive.

🖐 Make a list of some living and nonliving items that your child will be able to find in the backyard or another location appropriate for where you live. Give her the list and ask her to find the items, look at them, and decide if each one is a living or nonliving thing.

👁 Continue the original activity by flipping the page over and putting a nonliving thing on the other side.

👂 Ask your child to tell you about what living things need to live.

Mastery occurs when: your child can identify living and nonliving things and what distinguishes them.

You may want to help your child a little more if: she has trouble figuring out what makes things living. Make a list with your child of things that need food. Then add things that need water. Continue with things that need shelter and things that grow.

3 | Bird Feeder

Learning happens when: you read a book about birds with your child. Talk to him about what birds need to live. Make a pinecone bird feeder by tying string around one end of the pinecone, leaving enough extra string to tie the bird feeder to something outside. Smear peanut butter all over the pinecone, then roll it in birdseed. Tie the bird feeder to something outside, such as a tree branch, a balcony, or your windowsill.

TIME: 30 minutes

MATERIALS
▪ nonfiction book about birds
▪ pinecone
▪ string
▪ peanut butter
▪ birdseed

🖐 Have your child make a few extra pinecone bird feeders. Ask him to keep track of the kinds of birds that are eating the seeds on the pinecone. When the seeds start to get low, ask your child to hang another bird feeder.

👁 Watch the birds with your child. Keep track of what birds use the feeder. Try different types of seed and see if they attract different types of birds.

👂 Listen for the sounds each type of bird makes. After a while, see if your child can recognize the bird by the sound or if he can make the same sounds.

Mastery occurs when: your child is able to discuss with you and others what birds need to live.

You may want to help your child a little more if: he isn't able to recall what birds and other living things need to live. Try talking with your child about what he needs to live (food, water, shelter) and relating those needs to other living things. How would he feel without food or water for a day?

4 | Simple Machines

TIME: 30 minutes

MATERIALS
- paper
- pencils
- crayons

Learning happens when: you and your child talk about what a machine is. A simple machine is made of parts that can do things when put together that the individual parts cannot do by themselves. Walk around the yard or house to look for simple machines such as a pulley, a ramp, a bicycle, a window shade, and so on. Make a list of the simple machines that you find. Tell your child that you are not going to list anything that plugs into the wall or uses batteries or gas.

When you have listed fifteen or twenty things, talk about how to put them into categories, such as things I use, things my brother uses, and things the family uses, or things that help you clean, things that help you eat, things that help you go faster, and so on. Sometimes the only choice will be to list an item twice and/or to have a category of last resort—"other." Making the categories may be difficult for your child, and you should prompt her if she appears to be struggling. Ask her to rewrite the list as a chart by writing the names of the machines under each category. If you want, use a different color for the things in each category.

✍ Brainstorm ways to make a simple machine with your child. How can you make a ramp? What about a pulley?

👁 While you're out and about with your child, have her look for simple machines around town. What are the construction workers using to hoist bricks? How is the ramp helping make the delivery person's job easier?

👂 Have your child state the steps in order that are necessary to make a simple machine that you see in daily life.

Mastery occurs when: your child is able to identify and categorize simple machines.

You may want to help your child a little more if: she is unable to identify simple machines. Try laying out two or three things such as paper, a spoon, a manual can opener, and some kind of food. Which object is a machine? You may want to try this two or three times with different things. Then ask your child to find some more simple machines. If she has trouble categorizing the machines, make the categories for her and talk about what types of things should go in each category. Categorize the first couple of machines with your child and let her finish the chart.

5 | My Machine

TIME: 20 minutes

MATERIALS
- paper
- crayons

Learning happens when: you ask your child to design a machine on paper. You can let him make up any machine that he wants, or you can give him parameters, such as "Design a machine that stays in one place and cleans your whole room." Ask your child to write a sentence or two about the machine and then to read the sentences to you.

🖐 Collect all sorts of odds and ends, such as boxes, buttons, scraps, and so on, and have your child create a model of his machine.

👁 Go to a science museum with your child and find other simple machines. Ask him to read about each machine, look at it, and tell you what he read and saw.

👂 Go to a science museum, ask your child to listen to you or a guide describe what he is seeing, and restate it quietly to you.

Mastery occurs when: your child designs a machine that does something and he is able to tell you what it does.

You may want to help your child a little more if: he draws something that's not a machine or draws a machine but is unable to tell you about its parts or what it does.

6 | Parts of a Whole

Learning happens when: you give your child the toy or other simple machine to observe, operate, and take apart. Ask her to try to operate the toy as she takes each part off. Give her all the time that she wants. Talk about what each part does by itself and as part of the whole toy. Categorize the parts in different ways (by function, by color, by shape), then put them in order from most important to least important. Ask your child to write a sentence that tells what the toy does when all of the parts are put together and a sentence about what the toy does when the parts are not put together.

✋ Give your child some time and see if she can put the pieces back together to re-create the whole, or ask her to make a new machine from the pieces.

👁 Give your child a picture of a machine and ask her to draw the parts that she sees.

👂 Give your child a picture of a machine and ask her to tell you about the parts that she sees.

Mastery occurs when: your child identifies all of the parts that make up the whole toy and is able to categorize and order the parts according to different characteristics.

You may want to help your child a little more if: she is unable to identify all of the parts that make up the whole toy or is unable to categorize and order the parts according to different characteristics. Try doing the activity with your child, talking to her about each part and what functions it takes away from the whole as she takes it apart. Categorize and order the parts with your child, then ask her to try the activity again at another time.

Rocks, Soil, and Water

Finally, a reason to play in the mud, roll in the dirt, and get sand in your shoes. Your child will be taking a good look at rocks, soil, and water during first grade. As you have probably figured out, a lot of first grade is about sorting, classifying, and identifying attributes, including

TIME: 30 minutes

MATERIALS

▪ toy or other simple machine that your child can take apart (such as letting the air out of a ball, taking the wheels off a toy car, or taking apart a doll; be sure that the object comes apart easily and does not include any sharp parts inside)
▪ paper
▪ pencils

similarities and differences. Your child will observe and describe differences in rocks and soil samples, sort and classify rocks, observe soil components, investigate and compare sand particles of various sizes, and so on.

Rock, Soil, and Water Concepts	Having Problems?	Quick Tips
Describes differences between rocks and soil samples.	Is unable to describe differences between various rocks and soil samples.	Identify the differences between rocks and soil, then the similarities and differences between soil and sand.
Identifies how rocks, soil, and water are used.	Inconsistently identifies how rocks, soil, and water are used.	What is around you? Environmental learning is important for these concepts. It is easy to see how water is used, so start there. Things can be built with rocks, so learn that concept next. Save soil for last.
Identifies how rocks, soil, and water can be recycled.	Seems to be unaware of what can be recycled.	Try a hands-on project where you and your child take rocks from one place where they are not being used (the garden or driveway may be an example), then build something with them.
Identifies natural sources of water, including streams, lakes, and oceans.	Has difficulty identifying natural sources of water.	Talk about where water comes from and how it gets to you. Is a faucet in your house the place where water starts? No, it isn't. Is a rain cloud a place where water starts? Yes, it is.
Identifies similarities and differences in streams, lakes, and oceans.	Has difficulty distinguishing between streams, lakes, and oceans.	Help your child distinguish between bodies of water by talking about how you cross them. Do you cross the ocean the same way you cross a stream?

Once your child has examined, tested, described, and measured earth materials, she will go on to the uses and importance of soil, including describing and classifying organisms that live in the soil, particularly earthworms. Earthworms are good to study because they impact the soil in a positive way. Your child may also study other organisms that live in the soil.

From studying soil, your child will identify and describe a variety of natural sources of water, including streams, lakes, and oceans. She will be classifying and identifying attributes, including similarities and differences between the bodies of water. Finally, your child will be identifying how rocks, soil, and water are used and how they can be recycled. The table on page 136 describes some important concepts related to rocks, soil, and water, where children can run into problems, and what you can do to help them along.

Rock, Soil, and Water Activities

1 Dirt and Sand

Learning happens when: your child examines a small pile of soil and a small pile of sand. Ask him to describe them to you. Which one is softer? Which one would hold water and nutrients better? Can plants grow in sand? Can plants grow in soil? Which one is easier to walk on (if your child hasn't walked on sand, then ask him which one he thinks would be harder to walk on). Measure a cup of soil and a cup of sand. Put each sample in a plastic bag and seal the bags. Hold the plastic over the grains of sand and grains of dirt very tightly. Which is grainier? Is one heavier? Open the bags and smell the dirt and sand. Do they smell different? Pour

TIME: 30 minutes

MATERIALS
- soil (about a cup)
- sand (about a cup)
- plastic bags
- paper
- pencils
- magnifying glass

the sand and dirt out on the same surface but in different spots. Do they sound the same when landing on the surface? Clean them up off the surface. Is one of them harder to sweep up? Ask your child to record his observations on paper.

👋 Extend this activity by actually trying to grow things in both the soil and the sand. Let your child tend the plants and see what, if anything, sprouts. After a few weeks, discuss the findings.

👁 Look at the sand and the dirt through a magnifying glass. Talk about what they look like, then talk about grains of sand. Explain what a grain of sand is.

👂 Ask your child to hold dirt and then sand while telling you everything he can about its properties.

Mastery occurs when: your child identifies and records several properties—both similar and different—of the soil and the sand.

You may want to help your child a little more if: he is unable to describe the properties of soil and sand. Give him soil. Ask him specific questions about the soil. Measure the soil together. When your child is able to complete this activity with soil, try sand.

2 | Using the Earth

TIME: 30 minutes

MATERIALS
- paper
- pencils
- crayons or colored pencils

Learning happens when: you and your child talk about all of the ways we use soil, rock, and other earth materials in daily life. What is adobe? What is concrete? What is clay? Is there an adobe house or a stone walkway in the neighborhood? Do you have any clay pottery in the house? Brainstorm a list of at least five items made from earth materials. Rewrite the list as a chart by putting the items in categories, such as shelter, transportation, or decoration.

Ask your child to draw a picture of one of the things on the list, then write two sentences about the drawing.

Variations: Use earth materials to make things, then ask your child to write two sentences about what she made.

✋ Take a walk around the neighborhood with your child and look for examples of materials from the earth. How are they different? Do some have the same characteristics?

👁 Ask your child to write each item on the list on a separate index card. Mix up the cards, pick one, and ask her to locate a sample of that material around the house. Ask her to draw what she found and label the drawing.

👂 Describe a few different kinds of earth materials and see if your child can guess what each one is.

Mastery occurs when: your child can identify and describe earth materials and their uses in daily life.

You may want to help your child a little more if: she cannot identify and describe earth materials or cannot identify uses for those materials in daily life. Try walking around your neighborhood while talking about earth materials and their uses. Stop to touch, investigate, and talk about the soils and rocks that you see and the things that are made with them. Then try the activity again.

3 Rocks

Learning happens when: you give your child a few different rocks. Talk about their properties with your child. What colors are they? Are they porous (have holes that can hold water)? You can use a sponge as an example of something that's porous. How do the

TIME: 20 minutes

MATERIALS
- different types of rocks
- nontoxic glue
- various art supplies (for example, glitter, paint, markers, crayons, pipe cleaners)

properties of a natural rock help tell you about the earth in the area where you found it? Let your child choose a rock and decorate it.

Variations: Ask your child to tell you a story about where his favorite rock came from.

After looking at the rocks, create a rock garden with your child using a small box and some sand. Have your child arrange the rocks in whatever ways are attractive to him. Let your child add to the garden if he finds other rocks.

Go to a local rock shop, science store, or teacher supply store and get a geode or garnet and a small pick for your child. Let your child look at the stone and then crack it open. Geodes have beautiful crystals inside. Stones that have garnet in them are fun to observe because not only are they interesting, but kids can actually pick out the garnet with minimal effort and have a little treasure.

Read a book about rocks to your child. Ask him to tell you what he heard about rocks. Use this information to orally compare and contrast rocks and soil.

Mastery occurs when: your child identifies properties of different rocks and can describe them to you.

You may want to help your child a little more if: he is unable to describe different properties of rocks. Try asking your child to describe the properties of his favorite toy, pet, or room. Talk about using words that tell about things, then go back to the rocks later.

4 | Ocean Life

Learning happens when: you and your child read a book about oceans together. Then watch a movie with an ocean setting, play a computer game based on the ocean, play games with ocean toys in the tub, or go to the ocean or an aquarium if you can. Make it an ocean afternoon. Talk about the ocean habitat and how it is different from other habitats. How do fish breathe? (Through gills.) How do dolphins breathe? (They need to come up for air.) How do ocean plants live with no soil? Brainstorm a list of questions and research the answers together.

TIME: 2 hours (at least)

MATERIALS
■ book about oceans
■ other ocean information resources (such as videos, games, and sea creature toys)
■ paper
■ crayons

✋ Many aquariums have touch tanks where your child can pick up and hold some sea creatures.

👁 Watch a video, cartoon, or TV show that features ocean life. Ask your child to make a collage about ocean life using scraps of paper.

👂 Listen to a CD of ocean sounds and try to pick out the different sounds. Waves, dolphins, whales, and bubbles are common, although there are recordings of actual fish sounds as well.

Mastery occurs when: your child is able to describe some facts about ocean life, including how it is similar to and different from life on land.

You may want to help your child a little more if: she is unable to understand or describe concepts associated with ocean life. Try taking her to an aquarium or a pet store with fish. Talk about why fish have to live in aquariums and what else they need to live. Compare this environment to what other animals need to live. Try watching a TV show or movie that shows details about marine life.

5 It Lives in the Dirt

TIME: 45 minutes

MATERIALS
- book about worms, plants, ants, snakes, groundhogs, and/or other things that live in the dirt
- paper
- crayons

Learning happens when: you and your child read a book about something that lives in the dirt. Take a walk outside. If possible, spend some time digging in the dirt and talking about what you find.

✋ Start a small garden of potatoes or carrots with your child. Make sure he can identify the changes as the plants begin to grow. Have him help you tend the garden by watering and pulling out weeds. Point out the bugs and animals that could potentially harm the vegetables.

👁 Ask your child to draw pictures of things that live in the dirt. Let him eat some peanuts, potatoes, or something else that grows in the dirt while drawing and labeling the pictures.

👂 Read the book aloud to your child. Ask your child to tell you what he heard about the things that live in the ground. Use this information to compare and contrast things that live in the ground with things that live aboveground.

Mastery occurs when: your child can name some things that live in the earth.

You may want to help your child a little more if: he has trouble understanding that things live in the earth. Start by talking about animals that dig homes in the dirt, then move on to worms and other things that move around and get nutrients in the earth.

6 | Water Conservation

TIME: 10 minutes

Learning happens when: you and your child talk about water uses. Do you use water for brushing your teeth? Flushing the toilet? How about to clean your clothes? Water is important for drinking and cooking, too. What about helping plants grow?

How can you conserve water? Brainstorm with your child how your family can stop wasting water, such as fixing a leak or not leaving the faucet on while brushing your teeth. Post the list in a place where your family will be reminded to conserve water.

- Walk around the house with your child and see how many different ways your family uses water. If there's a leaky faucet that can be easily repaired, ask your child to help you fix it.

- Ask your child to illustrate a few ways to conserve water in your home.

- Play Guess That Water Sound. Blindfold your child. Carefully walk her around the house to different rooms where water is used: the sink, the dishwasher, and the ice machine in the kitchen; the toilet, the shower, and the sink in the bathroom; and so on. Let her try to guess by sound alone what you're using the water for.

Changes

Your first grader will spend time exploring many types of changes in the world. He will observe, measure, and record changes in size, mass, color, position, quantity, sound, and movement of a variety of objects and systems. First graders will observe and record changes in weather from day to day and over seasons, which leads to identifying and testing ways that heat may cause change, such as when ice melts.

Your child and his classmates will collect and record data about basic weather features including wind, temperature, precipitation, and cloud cover. First graders record weather observations and information on a weather calendar and use that information to compare data, identify possible trends, and form conclusions. Your child will learn to use observation and scientific information when forming pre-

Change Concepts	Having Problems?	Quick Tips
Observes and measures changes in size, color, position, and quantity.	Is unable to describe the changes that he or she sees.	Work with changes in quantity or color that involve food. First graders notice things like the color they are drinking and who has the most.
Observes and measures changes in sound and movement.	Is unable to identify the changes that occurred.	Driving in your car and listening to the radio gives you the perfect opportunity to talk about both changes in sound and how you measure the car's movement.
Identifies ways that heat may cause change, such as when ice melts at room temperature or when butter melts during cooking.	Is unable to identify the source of changes caused by heat.	Melting is a very easy concept to understand when whatever is melting is doing so in your hand. Move on to things that melt when cooked, then to other changes that happen with cooking.
Identifies changes in weather from day to day and over seasons.	Is unable to identify changes in the weather and seasonal weather.	Talk about the weather every day. Make it a routine. Ask your child about activities that are affected by the weather, such as "Wouldn't it be a good day to ice-skate?" or "Is it a good day to go swimming outside?"

dictions. On a practical level, he will begin to understand how weather affects our lives.

Tadpoles and butterflies are excellent examples of life cycle changes for first graders. Other good examples of changes are:

- Things that melt in the sun
- Day and night
- Cooking changes, particularly popcorn
- Changing liquid to ice and ice to liquid
- Changing weather

The table on page 144 describes some important concepts related to changes, where children can run into problems, and what you can do to help them along.

Change Activities

1 Weather Watching

Learning happens when: you and your child take some time to talk about the weather each day. Make or buy a calendar with squares big enough to write on. If you have an outdoor thermometer, ask your child to record the temperature each day (or every other day) for an extended period of time (ideally for more than one season).

TIME: 5 minutes daily

MATERIALS
- calendar
- markers or pencils

Make a big chart to keep track of the weather and its changes. Decide with your child how to categorize the data. Will you use stickers, markers, or crayons? Will you use actual pictures of weather that you cut out?

👁 Start a weather binder with your child. Each day at roughly the same time, ask him to see what the weather is like outside and draw it on a sheet of paper to put in the binder.

👂 Ask your child for the morning weather report before he gets a chance to ask you. Is it going to be sunny? Is it going to be cold? Are you going to need boots or an umbrella? Let him check the thermometer and the radio, TV, or newspaper for the most updated information, then share it at the breakfast table before leaving for the day.

Mastery occurs when: your child consistently measures and records weather data.

You may want to help your child a little more if: he is unable to consistently measure and record weather data.

2 | Forms of Corn

TIME: 10 minutes

MATERIALS
- popcorn
- measuring cup
- paper
- crayons or markers

Learning happens when: you and your child look at some unpopped corn. Would it be good to eat? Prepare a batch of popcorn and compare it to the unpopped corn. How did popping change the corn? Talk about all of the changes that popping did to the corn—the size, the color, the way it feels, the smell. What noise did it make when it was changing? What caused the changes? (Heat.) Ask your child to make a chart using one color of crayon or marker to list observations for unpopped corn and another color to list the observations of popped corn.

✋ Ask your child to hold the popped and unpopped corn while comparing and contrasting them orally.

👁 Provide written directions about how to do the activity for your child and ask her to read and follow them.

Corn makes noise when it changes or pops. This is perfect for learners who associate sounds with facts. What other things did your child hear? Ask her to describe her observations that feature the senses.

Mastery occurs when: your child is able to compare and contrast the popped and unpopped corn while understanding that heat caused the changes.

You may want to help your child a little more if: she is unable to compare and contrast the popped and unpopped corn or understand that heat caused the changes to the corn. Try putting the corn in the freezer. Did it pop? Leave it on the counter. Did it pop? Try popping the corn the right way. What caused the corn to finally pop?

3 Drinking Changes

Learning happens when: you give your child a small amount of two kinds of powdered drink mix. Let him mix and match small amounts of each kind. What happens to the color of the powder? What happens to the smell and the taste? Put each mixture into a numbered paper cup. Ask your child to write his observations about the mixtures in each cup. Add water, then write down more observations. Let your mad scientist make as many potions as he wants, but make sure that he records observations about the changes that each potion exhibits.

TIME: 20 minutes

MATERIALS
- 2 kinds of powdered drink mix
- measuring cup and spoons
- paper cups
- paper
- pencils

Try this activity with powdered gelatin mixes. Ask your child to demonstrate the experiment to you.

Use red, yellow, and blue powdered drink mixes and let your child make all the colors of the rainbow. Make sure he can tell you which colors mix to make others.

🎧 Ask your child to tell you how to make the best-flavored drink mix. How much of each flavor did he use? How did he come up with those amounts?

Mastery occurs when: your child makes a variety of potions and records the changes to the color, taste, smell, and other observations.

You may want to help your child a little more if: he is unable to record the changes to the color, taste, smell, and other observations. Try recording the changes in color and taste (the most obvious changes) before moving on to more discrete observations.

4 | The Life Stages of a Butterfly

TIME: 60 minutes

MATERIALS
▪ book about butterflies and their life cycle
▪ paper
▪ crayons

Learning happens when: you and your child talk about the way some animals change a lot and some animals don't change much as they grow up. Read a book about butterflies to your child. Does a young butterfly look the same as a grown butterfly? Talk about the life stages of a butterfly. Here are the major concepts:

- Larvae and caterpillars need food, air, and a place to live and grow.
- The caterpillar forms a chrysalis, which is a protective covering.
- A butterfly emerges from the chrysalis.
- A butterfly needs food to live, but it does not grow after emerging from the chrysalis.

The life cycle is completed when a butterfly lays eggs, which hatch into larvae. Show pictures of the process and have your child draw them. Label the stages that the butterfly goes through.

Ask your child to tell you about her personal experiences with butterflies.

Variations: Extend this lesson to include art and math by making a symmetrical piece of butterfly art.

Go outside and see if you and your child can find examples of animals or insects in various stages of change. Generally the best time to do this is in the spring, although depending on where you live, you can find animals and insects that change in the late fall to early winter.

Take some pictures of the critters that are in your own backyard. Keep an eye on them throughout the year and take pictures as they change. Caterpillars are great for this!

Ask your child to record herself talking about the life cycle of a butterfly. Listen to the recording with her and talk about it.

Mastery occurs when: your child is able to correctly identify and describe the different life stages of a butterfly.

You may want to help your child a little more if: she is unable to identify each organism as a butterfly in a different life stage. Try talking with her about other organisms' life stages and relating them back to the butterfly. If your child simply has trouble with the order of the butterfly's life stages, go over them again and talk about how they look.

5 | Mothers and Babies

Learning happens when: you and your child read the book about mothers and babies. Talk about the book as you are reading. Ask your child to show you what he knows about mothers and babies by matching the pictures of mothers to their babies.

TIME: 30 minutes

MATERIALS
■ book about animal mothers and babies, such as *Are You My Mother?* or *Blueberries for Sal*
■ pictures of animal mothers and babies (you can find pictures of mothers and babies to print at www. knowledgeessentials.com)

✋ Play Memory or Concentration. Make cards with pictures of mothers and babies, flip them facedown, then try to match mothers to babies.

👁 Watch a video about mothers and babies. Talk with your child about which animal babies look most like their mothers. Which babies look the least like their mothers?

👂 How do you and your child communicate? Mostly by talking but also with body language. Get a video or a book about how different animals communicate with their young and read it with your child.

Mastery occurs when: your child correctly associates the pictures of mothers with the pictures of their babies.

You may want to help your child a little more if: he is unable to associate the pictures of mothers with their babies. Talk to him about how offspring usually look like their parents. Human babies look like humans, gorilla babies look like gorillas, and so forth.

Environmental Learning

Science is a very natural topic to talk about in your daily life. The weather is one of the most commonly talked about subjects: Is there a pattern to the weather? What season is it? What holidays happen in this season? Talk about what to wear in each type of weather.

Systems, changes, earth materials, and life cycles are integral parts of daily life. It is easy to talk about them with your child in ways that keep his interest. It is easiest to learn and remember new concepts if you are discovering them when they mean something to you. Talking to your child about life cycles and changes when he just found a tadpole is far more effective than sitting your child down at a table to learn about them.

End of First Grade Science Checklist

Students who are working at the standard level at the end of first grade:

____ Identify and describe bodies of water and marine life

____ Can make observations and recognize similarities and differences

____ Categorize living and nonliving things and systems

____ Understand that there are a variety of earth materials

____ Describe life stages, particularly of a butterfly or a tadpole

First Grade Social Studies 9

Beginning of First Grade Social Studies Checklist

Students who are working at the standard level at the beginning of first grade:

_____ Identify rules that must be followed at home and at school

_____ Know some holidays

_____ Understand that they live in a town/community/city

_____ Know the components of their families

There is much more to social studies than meets the eye. It is the class in which your little angel is taught that a bigger world exists than what is on her street and that there are rules you have to follow when you are out there. Your child will learn to be a good citizen of the world by studying history and appreciating other cultures.

Have you ever heard a teacher ask a child who is breaking the rules if he thinks he is being a good citizen? That teacher is reinforcing the concept that we respect the rights of others. The cornerstone is the ability to follow rules. Rules are in place to limit behaviors that infringe on the rights of others, for safety reasons, or to ensure that all people in a group are treated equitably. Rules are an important cog in the wheel of our society. Consistently enforcing them at school and at home is an important component of your child's first grade social studies education.

Another important topic in first grade social studies covers what national symbols are and what they stand for, and when national holidays are and why we celebrate them. Understanding national symbols and holidays helps relate things in our country to history, building your child's understanding that:

- Things around him have been here for a long time.

- There are individuals who we consider to be so admirable and important to our nation's history that we celebrate them, such as Abraham Lincoln or Martin Luther King Jr.

- Events in our past have made a difference in how things are for us right now, such as Columbus discovering America or the Pilgrims settling here.

- We use symbols to represent ideals for our society, such as the stars and stripes or the bald eagle.

Learning about the United States is the primary focus of many first grade social studies lessons, but your child will also spend time learning that people live in a lot of different ways both in the United States and in the rest of the world and that we keep track of these places on maps.

First grade classes will often alternate social studies and science lessons (by day or month), and they are usually in the afternoon.

Civics

You know the three branches of government, checks and balances, and how a bill becomes a law. Now I bet you are wondering, civics for first graders? Yes, civics begins in first grade with the concept of being a good citizen. As part of civics, first graders begin to explore the broad concepts of rights and responsibilities in the world around them. The classroom serves as a microcosm of society in which decisions are made with a sense of individual responsibility, respect for other people, and adherence to basic social rules, such as fair play, good sportsmanship, and respecting the rights and opinions of others. Your job is to extend that microcosm to the home. Talk to your child about the rules you follow in different situations, such as when you drive a car. Why do we have these rules? What would happen if we didn't have them?

Civics Concepts	Having Problems?	Quick Tips
Identifies characteristics of good citizenship.	Doesn't understand that one person's actions affect the people around him.	Litterbug! Take one characteristic of citizenship at a time, such as putting trash in the proper place. What happens when you don't?
Knows historic figures who have exemplified good citizenship, such as Betsy Ross, George Washington, and Abraham Lincoln.	Doesn't realize that the actions of people in the past who were good citizens affect our daily lives now.	Read stories about people in history who have been good citizens and talk about them. How do their actions from the past affect us today?
Identifies when ordinary people are good citizens.	Does not recognize actions people do every day that make them good citizens.	Focus on one thing, such as standing in line. Why do people stand in line? Whose rights are being respected when we stand in line? Are people in the line being good citizens? How do people break the rules about lines (for example, using the express lane at the store when they have too many items or cutting in line)?

This table describes some important concepts related to civics, where children can run into problems, and what you can do to help them along.

Civics Activities

1 Mother, May I?

Learning happens when: you and your child play the game Mother, May I? Your child and maybe some of his friends stand on the opposite side of the yard (or room) from you within hearing distance. You say a command, such as "Take six baby steps forward!" Your child must ask, "Mother, may I?" before taking the six steps. You respond, "Yes, you may." If a child moves without asking or before you say, "Yes, you may," he or she must go back to the

TIME: 15 minutes

starting line. Make sure you include lots of different movements that have a forward motion, such as walking, running, hopping, jumping, galloping, sliding, leaping, and skipping. Also include movements that don't include a forward motion, such as bending, straightening, curling, stretching, twisting, turning, swinging, swaying, rising, and collapsing. Try combining the types of movements. When the first child reaches you, he or she wins.

Variations: Respond either "Yes, you may" or "No, you may not."

✋ This activity is perfect for the child who likes to be on the move.

👁 Show your child how the game is played while you are telling him.

👂 Trade places with your child and let him be the leader. Brainstorm some actions that he can call out for you to do.

Mastery occurs when: your child enjoys the game and plays by the rules.

You may want to help your child a little more if: he compulsively moves before asking, "Mother, may I?" Try decreasing the distance and give him very simple commands.

2 Board Game

TIME: 45 minutes

MATERIALS
▪ board game that is unfamiliar to your child; try to use a game within your child's age range, as indicated on the game

Learning happens when: you give the game to your child without telling her how to play. Give her time to explore the game, including looking at the directions. After a few minutes, ask her to tell you how to play. After your child has completed her instructions, you should correct her directions if needed. Play the game with your child. Talk about the importance of following the directions and rules of the game. Ask her how it feels to play with someone who doesn't follow the rules. When you are finished playing the game, ask her to make a list of times when it is important to follow rules. This activity is also a reading comprehension activity, so feel free to double up the concepts that you are working on in one sitting. Let this be the way you and your child explore all new games.

Variations: Let your child make up her own rules and tell them to you. Does the game work that way?

- Before you correct your child's instructions, play the game her way. Did it work? Why or why not?
- Rewrite the directions with your child's help on a large sheet of paper with markers or crayons.
- Read the directions to your child and ask her to tell them back to you.

Mastery occurs when: your child is able to understand most of the rules of the game by simply looking at the game pieces and reading the directions. If she is successfully able to identify the importance of rules, she comprehends why rules are listed for the game.

You may want to help your child a little more if: she is not able to understand most of the rules of the game on her own. Explain the game to her and play it; then choose a simpler game and retry the activity.

3 Rules of the Road

Learning happens when: you and your child brainstorm to create a list of all the traffic rules you know. Make a list of them that you can post in your child's room. Walk with him to school, to the

TIME: 30 minutes

MATERIALS
- poster board, dry erase board, or large sheet of paper
- markers
- bicycle (optional)
- bicycle helmet (optional)

local park, and around your neighborhood while you are talking to him about the rules that pedestrians, bicyclists, and cars follow so that everyone is safe. Introduce your child to the school crossing guards, show him the pedestrian traffic light, and use the crosswalk with him.

If your child will be riding his bike to school, ride there with him a few times before he rides alone. (He should ride alone only if you feel comfortable.) Practice bike safety on the ride and park the bike in the bike rack or other area designated for leaving bikes. If your child will be riding the subway to school, now is the time to reinforce the safe riding rules that you probably already observe.

Talk about bus safety with your child. Even if he doesn't ride the bus every day, he will ride school buses for field trips. Talk about traffic safety when you are driving. Go back to the list that you brainstormed earlier and talk about the rules on the list. When did your child see you follow a safety rule? When did he follow a safety rule? Discuss the reasons for rules. Are there any rules that need to be added to the list? If so, add them. Continue reinforcing the safety rules often, but don't try to scare your child into following the rules.

- Take a walk with your child around the neighborhood. Ask him to point out signs, people, and other things that help keep you safe in traffic, such as crosswalks, crossing guards, and so on.

- If your child learns best visually, take a drive in the car and ask him to point out the safety rules that are appropriate.

- Talk with your child about noises associated with safety. What noises in the house help keep you safe? (Smoke alarm, security alarm.) What about outside? (Police siren, honking horns.)

Mastery occurs when: your child is able to remember safety rules without being reminded and comprehends the need for the rules.

You may want to help your child a little more if: he is unable to remember safety rules without being reminded or doesn't comprehend the need for the rules.

4 School Rules

Learning happens when: you and your child sit down and read the school handbook together. Most schools require that you do this during the first week of school, and it is important that you actually do it. It will make you and your child aware of the rules so that you will both be more comfortable in the school environment.

TIME: 60 minutes

MATERIALS
your school's handbook

- If your child is a kinesthetic learner, you should incorporate a movement, such as clapping or snapping, when she hears an important rule.
- If your child is a visual learner, list the rules that are most important to remember.
- If your child is an auditory learner, list the most important rules and ask her to read them aloud to you (or read them aloud together) on a daily basis during the first month of school.

Mastery occurs when: you and your child are able to follow the school rules without having to be reminded.

You may want to help your child a little more if: she has problems following the school rules without being reminded. Practice the rules with her in a variety of ways, such as making flash cards, role-playing, reading the rules aloud, and explaining why they are important.

5 | Make the Signs

TIME: 45 minutes

MATERIALS
- paper
- rounded-edge scissors
- crayons or markers

Learning happens when: you and your child brainstorm a list of the traffic and pedestrian safety signs that you have seen together. Talk about what each of the signs looks like and what each of the signs means. Leave the list in a place where your child can see it. You may write what each sign on the list means and some of the characteristics of the sign (for example, red means stop). Let your child choose one or two of the signs to make.

- Take a walk around the block and see how many signs there are. What do they mean? How do they help keep you safe?

- Ask your child to make or draw pictures of all of the signs on your list.

- While driving, point out signs and ask your child to tell you what they mean.

Mastery occurs when: your child contributes significantly to the brainstorming session and makes his signs correctly.

You may want to help your child a little more if: he is unable to identify many signs on his own. Try taking a walk or a drive to see some of the signs again before starting this activity. Talk about what each sign looks like and what each sign means.

National Symbols and Holidays

National symbols are pretty easy to teach first graders because they are learning the name of an object or an event—very concrete, very first grade. It is always best to talk about things as children see them or when they come up in conversations, such as introducing the Statue of

Liberty or Ellis Island when children see pictures of them. Talk about the flag when you pass it in your community. The more you introduce subjects or behaviors when they are happening, the more attention you will have from your little one.

The bald eagle is another great symbol to talk about, and it gives you an opportunity to discuss endangered species, conservation, habitats, and migration. Your state has symbols, such as the state flag, state bird, state flower, state tree, state song, and state slogan. You can find a link to your state information at www.knowledgeessentials.com.

To a first grader, the best holidays involve presents and/or candy, the second best holidays involve school parties, the third best holidays are the ones where you get out of school, and the other holidays are hard to remember. Holidays that we celebrate in the United States include the national holidays, as well as those that vary according to region, religion, and tradition. Each state has its own state holidays (Statehood Day, Land Run Day in Oklahoma, and others). You should become familiar with your state holidays and talk to your child about why the people in your state celebrate them. Generally, first graders learn about:

New Year's Eve and Day

President's Day

Mother's Day

Memorial Day

Father's Day

Independence Day

Labor Day

Columbus Day

Thanksgiving

National Events and Holidays Concepts	Having Problems?	Quick Tips
Explains selected national and state patriotic symbols, such as the American flag and your state flag.	Can't identify and describe even a few patriotic symbols.	Draw a few of the symbols on index cards and write their names on other cards, then play Memory. Every time you see a state or national symbol, talk about it and why it is important.
Understands the value of using voting as a way of making choices and decisions that are the most fair to the most people.	Isn't concerned with experiencing the fairest outcome for the most people.	Vote, vote, vote! Take your child with you to the polls when voting in local, state, and national elections. Vote on what to have for dinner. Voting is important—do it and talk about it often.

This table describes some important concepts related to national symbols and holidays, where children can run into problems, and what you can do to help them along.

National Symbols and Holiday Activities

 National Holiday Scramble

TIME: 20 minutes

MATERIALS
- index cards
- markers

Learning happens when: you write the name of each national holiday on an index card. Next, write something that is done to celebrate or commemorate each holiday on index cards. Put the index cards of the holidays in rows faceup. Put the other index cards in different rows facedown. Let your child pick an index card that is facedown and match it with the holiday. Start with these national holidays:

President's Day

Memorial Day

Independence Day

Labor Day

Columbus Day

Thanksgiving

Ask your child to talk about the holiday and any special memories of the holiday when he has a successful match.

Variations: Try adding other holidays to the game.

✋ Place the descriptive index cards facedown on one side of the room and the holiday name cards on the other side of the room. Time your child as he chooses a descriptive card, then runs across the room to match it to the proper holiday name card.

👁 Write the names of the holidays, then show your child actual objects or photos that coincide with the holidays. Ask him to match the words to the objects or photos.

🎵 Music to your ears! Many holidays have music that relates to them. Pick holidays with distinctive music and use the music instead of cards to see if your child can make the connection.

Mastery occurs when: your child is able to name our national holidays and describe why or how we celebrate them while playing this game.

You may want to help your child a little more if: he is unable to name our national holidays and describe why or how we celebrate them. Spend some time matching the holidays with him and talking about basic facts associated with the holidays before trying the activity again.

2 | Flag Day Any Day

TIME: 30 minutes

MATERIALS
- red, white, and blue construction paper
- rounded-edge scissors
- white crayon
- square pattern
- nontoxic glue
- pencils

Learning happens when: you and your child talk about the flag and why we have one. Point out that every country has its own flag and that every state has its own flag. Talk about what the American flag looks like. What are the shapes and what are the colors? Tell your child what the stars, stripes, and colors stand for:

- Red means hardiness and valor.

- White signifies purity and innocence.

- Blue represents vigilance and justice.

- The stars symbolize heaven.

- There is one star for every state in the union.

- The stripes are rays of light from the sun.

- There are thirteen stripes because that is how many states were in the union when the first flag was made.

Let your child make a flag by starting with a piece of blue paper and tracing the square in the upper left corner. Let her draw 50 five-pointed stars (or five groups of ten) in the square that she traced. Cut the strips of paper that will be the stripes next: the flag has thirteen stripes—six white stripes and seven red stripes—with a red stripe at the top and at the bottom. Cut shorter stripes for the ones that go by the stars. Glue the stripes in place.

Variations: Ask your child to write a fact about the flag on each stripe.

✍ Do a little research with your child either at the library or on the Internet to find out information about your state flag. When was your state founded? What number state was it? What symbols are used on your state flag and why?

👁 If your child learns better by seeing things, take her outside to see an American flag, either at your house or at any school or government building. See if she can point out all the important aspects of the flag.

👂 Ask your child to sing songs that she knows about the flag, such as "Grand Old Flag" or "The Star-Spangled Banner."

Mastery occurs when: your child successfully makes a flag while learning about what the flag symbolizes.

You may want to help your child a little more if: she has trouble making the flag. Work with her on the mechanics of putting the flag together while you talk about what the flag symbolizes.

3 | Birds! Birds! Birds!

Learning happens when: you find out what your official state bird is and get a picture of it. (If you have Internet access, go to www.knowledgeessentials.com.) Find out why it is your state bird. What kinds of things does it need in its habitat to survive? Tell your child this information as he makes the bird out of construction paper, or let him draw the bird if that's what he prefers. Ask your child to tell you about the bird after he has made one.

Variations: Add our national bird, the bald eagle, to the activity. Add birds from other states where friends or family live.

TIME: 20 minutes

MATERIALS
- construction paper
- crayons
- rounded-edge scissors
- nontoxic glue

✋ Find out what types of food your state bird eats. Set up a bird feeder in your yard to see if you can spot one.

👁 Grab binoculars and go bird-watching with your child to see if you can find your state bird.

👂 Go online to find out what your state bird sounds like.

Research the bird's nesting habits with your child and have him tell you about them.

Mastery occurs when: your child learns about his state bird.

You may want to help your child a little more if: he doesn't learn about the state bird. Try presenting the information in a more straightforward manner without the arts and crafts project.

4 Local Landmarks

TIME: 30–60 minutes

MATERIALS
- paper
- pencils

Learning happens when: you and your child take a walk around your community to see the historical sites and/or local landmarks. This can be done a little at a time over a week or so, or you can look at them all in one day. If your community has no special landmarks, show your child the city or town hall, the city limits or town borderlines, your local places of worship, or the park.

As you and your child look at the local landmarks, talk about why they are important to the community. What are the types of things that communities like to build to remember someone or something? Are there certain things that you will find in every town (such as a post office)? Talk about them. Ask your child to choose a landmark and write four sentences about it. Ask her to read the sentences to you or another family member.

Variations: Make this activity a routine that you follow when learning about new communities.

✋ It's everyone's community—help keep it nice! Volunteer with your child to help clean up a park or other community area.

👁 If you're allowed to, take photos of important landmarks, buildings, or other points of interest for your child. Ask her to label the pictures and write a sentence about each one.

See if there are any tours of important landmarks in your community, such as the city hall or municipal buildings. You can also go to your local library or historical records building to hear about historical landmarks in your community. After the tour, ask your child to retell the facts that she learned about your community.

Mastery occurs when: your child is able to recall facts about local landmarks and talk about them with you.

You may want to help your child a little more if: she is unable to recall basic facts about landmarks in your community. Continue to point out the landmarks and talk about them when out and about with your child.

5   Personal Holiday

Learning happens when: you and your child talk about why we celebrate holidays. Ask him to think of a new holiday that we should all celebrate and why he thinks this holiday would be a good one. Why would it be important to celebrate? Ask your child to tell you when and how that holiday would be celebrated. What kinds of decorations would people use for the holiday? Would there be greeting cards? What would the cards say? Ask him to write some sentences on the lined paper that tell about his holiday.

Variations: Try celebrating your child's holiday at your house.

Let your child create some of the decorations that go with his holiday. While he is working, ask him about the significance of the decorations. Do they have a meaning? Do they symbolize something?

TIME: 30 minutes

MATERIALS
- lined paper
- drawing paper
- pencils
- crayons or markers

👁 Ask your child to draw a few pictures to illustrate his sentences about the new holiday.

👂 Gather up the family for the first telling of the story of your child's holiday. Where did the holiday come from? Why should the family celebrate it?

Mastery occurs when: your child is able to think about and create a holiday that focuses on people other than himself, meaning he has comprehended the reasons why we celebrate holidays.

You may want to help your child a little more if: he can think only of holidays that are focused on personal events, such as his birthday or another event that marks a milestone in his life. You should spend more time talking about the different kinds of holidays that people celebrate either in your community, in the United States, or around the world. What makes an event significant enough that a lot of people want to celebrate it? Ask your child to think about what kind of holiday he would create again while keeping in mind the things you talked about.

Communities and Cultures

Teaching your child about communities of people and the way they live will set the tone for not only how your child interacts with the people around him but also how he chooses to resolve conflicts when they arise.

Families and family roles are defined for first graders in social studies. Children talk about characteristics of their own families and compare them to characteristics of others, both in the United States and in other countries. Characteristics include size, composition, roles and responsibilities, languages, religions, food, housing, traditions, and type of government. As children identify these characteristics, they talk

Community and Culture Concepts	Having Problems?	Quick Tips
Describes ways that families meet basic human needs.	Is unable to identify appropriate basic needs.	If you are an outdoorsy family, camping is a great demonstration of meeting basic needs. If you are city dwellers, make a point of discussing basic needs at appropriate times (at the grocery store, when you are going to work, etc.).
Describes similarities and differences in ways families meet basic human needs.	Is unable to describe ways that families meet basic needs.	Once your child is able to identify that the resources around you are important to meeting basic needs, you can move on to comparing how other families meet basic needs. For example, people who live on farms or in the mountains meet basic needs differently from those who live in cities or by the ocean.
Describes various beliefs, customs, and traditions of families and communities and explains their importance.	Is unable to describe various beliefs, customs, and traditions of families and communities.	Discussion is important in helping your child identify customs and traditions that are prevalent in your community. Pick one custom that your family and community participate in and talk about its purpose, historical roots, and importance.

about which are influenced by the natural environment (for example, would you find a beach house in Wyoming?). Children are taught to recognize and value diversity among different cultures.

In looking at communities, first graders look at different workers in communities, similarities and differences between communities, and their own role in the community. You can start introducing these concepts when talking about the rules of the road by introducing your child to the crossing guard and pointing out police officers and other community helpers. Talk about the communities that other family members live in and other communities that you have visited. How are those communities the same and how are they different?

The table on page 169 describes important concepts related to communities and cultures, where children can run into problems, and what you can do to help them along.

Community and Culture Activities

1 Family Tree

TIME: 30 minutes

MATERIALS
■ large sheet of paper (such as a paper grocery bag, poster board, construction paper, or drawing paper)
■ crayons or markers

Learning happens when: you draw a tree trunk with branches up the middle of the paper. Draw two lines on one side of the top of the tree. Tell your child to write his maternal grandparents' names on these lines. Draw two lines on the other side of the top of the tree for your child to write the names of his paternal grandparents. Talk to your child about what to write on the lines, and let him use the names that he calls his grandparents. Help him count how many aunts and uncles he has on your side of the family. He should fill in their names on lines under the appropriate grandparents.

Help your child count how many aunts and uncles he has on the other parent's side of the family so that he can fill in their names under the appropriate grandparents. Help your child fill in the names of his cousins and brothers and sisters underneath the rows of aunts and uncles and parents.

✋ Let your child interact with the materials by sorting family pictures to go on the tree, grouping them in a couple of ways before deciding how to make the tree.

👁 If your child learns better visually, try this activity with photos.

Once your child has made the tree, have a family gathering to share his work. Ask your child to tell everyone how he made the tree and what it shows.

Mastery occurs when: your child can correctly identify the members of his immediate and extended family and understands how they are related.

You may want to help your child a little more if: he is unable to correctly identify the members of his immediate and extended family and their relationships. You may want to start with just your immediate family.

2 Family Stories

Learning happens when: you sit with your child and tell her a family story. Talk about whether the story is true. Are parts of it true and other parts exaggerated? Talk about how true stories can become tall tales. Let your child add to the story to make it a tall tale or an even taller tale.

TIME: 20 minutes

Variations: Let your child draw pictures that go with the story, write her own version of the story, or act out the story.

Walk around a place that is significant to your family. Talk with your child about why it's so important to the family story.

Share old family photos while talking about the family story. This gives your visual learner something to relate to when hearing the story.

After sharing the story with your child and discussing how to exaggerate it, try taping your child telling the story so that she can share it with other family members.

Mastery occurs when: your child understands the nature of family stories and family tall tales.

You may want to help your child a little more if: she is not interested in family stories. Try telling a story that involves her (for example, "When you were just a baby . . ."). Talk to her about whether other people in the family might like to hear the story. You might tell her that more people will be interested in her stories if she is interested in theirs.

3 | Community Here or There?

TIME: 30 minutes

MATERIALS
■ index cards
■ markers

Write the names of two or more types of communities (such as city, town, farm, rural, urban) on index cards and the names of community features (such as subways, tractors, fields, parks, a stadium, many people, few people) on other index cards.

Learning happens when: you place the community cards faceup and give your child the index cards that have community features written on them. Ask him to read the words on each card aloud, then match the card with the features to the right communities. Features that are in every community can go in any row. Your child should place that card above the name of the community he is choosing. He will end up making rows that look like a bar graph.

Variations: If your child is familiar with specific diverse communities, then list those by name and ask him to match the features to those places.

✋ Ask your child to build a model of your community with blocks or other materials.

👁 Ask your child to go through magazines and find pictures that can be associated with each community.

🔊 Use the community features cards as clues to help your auditory learner. Give your child the cards with the communities on them. Say one clue from the community features card every few seconds. When your child thinks he knows what community you're talking about, have him throw down the card.

Mastery occurs when: your child successfully matches the features cards to the right community.

You may want to help your child a little more if: he has trouble matching the features cards to the right community. Try giving him an index card with one type of community written on it. Brainstorm all of the things you can think of about this community and write them on the cards. Do the same thing for another type of community, then try the activity again.

4 | Community Helper Charades

Write the names of several kinds of community helpers (such as police officer, doctor, postal carrier, firefighter, teacher, pastor) on the small sheets of paper. Fold the papers and put them into the bag.

TIME: 20 minutes

MATERIALS
- small sheets of paper
- pencils
- bag

Learning happens when: you let your child choose one of the sheets of paper and act out what the helper on the piece of paper does.

Variations: Let your child choose a piece of paper, then say one word that describes the helper. Try to guess which helper she is describing.

✋ Help your child to create mini-dramas about the helper. Maybe she can pretend to deliver mail—all she needs is some paper and envelopes and a satchel to put them in. Selecting the right props always gets the imagination going!

👁 Ask your child to draw on individual index cards different things that each helper would use. Mix up the cards. Say the name of a helper to your child, then ask her to find the cards that have things that person would use.

👂 If your child is a great listener, every five seconds give her a word that relates to one of the helpers. Continue until she can identify the helper.

Mastery occurs when: your child successfully identifies key characteristics of community helpers.

You may want to help your child a little more if: she is unable to identify key characteristics of community helpers. Spend more time discussing these helpers and what they do. Ask her to draw pictures of the helpers at a time when they are helping. Look at the picture to see if your child has an accurate perception of this community member before trying the activity again.

Environmental Learning

The environment is often the most appropriate place to discuss the concepts your child is learning at school, and first grade social studies is ripe for environmental learning. There is no better place to talk about the community than when you are in your community. When you are driving, talk about the rules of the road. When someone is behaving as a good citizen or a poor citizen, talk about that. When you go to vote, talk about why you are voting. Why should you recycle? Why not litter? You model proper social behavior on a daily basis, and you can help your child learn to do this on a more regular basis if you talk about why, when, how, and what you are doing as a good citizen of your community.

The holidays are another perfect subject for environmental learning—built-in times to introduce and reinforce the social, historic, and personal impacts of holidays that you celebrate. Don't be afraid to impart your years of wisdom to your child—social studies is an area where you can do it in a natural and effective way.

End of First Grade Social Studies Checklist

Students who are working at the standard level at the end of first grade:

_____ Know the name of their country

_____ Know the name of their state

_____ Know and follow school and community rules

_____ Understand that there are places with special meaning to people, usually called landmarks

_____ Name and understand the meanings of major U.S. holidays

Teaching Your First Grader Thinking Skills

10

Teaching your first grader to think sounds like a lofty goal, doesn't it? You can help foster a thinking mind in your child by treating him or her as an active participant in a home where you explore "why" and "how" questions. The more opportunities your child has to explore ideas and be heard at home, the more likely he or she is to be an active thinker both in and out of school.

> ## Beginning of First Grade Thinking Skills Checklist
>
> Students working on the standard level at the beginning of first grade:
>
> _____ Are moving toward abstract thinking
>
> _____ Are developing reasoning skills
>
> _____ Have difficulty making choices

Teaching children to think reasonably and logically improves children's impulsive behavior and social adjustment. Children taught this way are less likely to develop behavioral difficulties than are well-adjusted children who do not learn these skills. Of course, the way you respond to your child and act in front of him or her makes the largest impact on how your child learns to think and communicate.

In a study of children from kindergarten through fourth grade (Shure, 1993) that was the culmination of twenty years of research to test ideas about thinking skills, parent modeling, and behavior, M. B. Shure delineated four levels of communication that we use all the time:

LEVEL 1: POWER ASSERTION (DEMANDS, BELITTLES, PUNISHES)

- Do it because I say so!
- Do you want a time out?
- How many times have I told you . . . !
- If you can't share the truck, I'll take it away so that neither of you will have it.

LEVEL 2: POSITIVE ALTERNATIVE (NO EXPLANATION)

- I'm on the phone now. Go watch TV.
- Ask him for the truck.
- You should share your toys.

LEVEL 3: INDUCTION (EXPLANATIONS AND REASONS)

- I feel angry when you interrupt me.
- If you hit, you'll lose a friend (hurt him).
- You'll make him angry if you hit him (grab toys).
- You shouldn't hit (grab). It's not nice.

LEVEL 4: PROBLEM-SOLVING PROCESS (TEACHING THINKING)

- What's the problem? What's the matter?
- How do you think I (she/he) feel(s) when you hit (grab)?
- What happened (might happen) when you did (do) that?
- Can you think of a different way to solve this problem (tell him/her/me how you feel)?
- Do you think that is or is not a good idea? Why (why not)?

The parents who communicated as often as possible on level 4 in Shure's study had children who were the least impulsive, the least withdrawn, and showed the fewest behavior problems as observed by independent raters.

We all know that there are times when communicating on level 1 is the only way to go, so don't beat yourself up. You can't reason a child out of the street when a car is coming. Awareness of the communication levels enables you to implement the highest level as much of the time as possible, which in turn fosters a thinking child.

Teaching and modeling thinking encourages children to ask questions about information and ideas. It helps your child learn how to identify unstated assumptions, form and defend opinions, and see relationships between events and ideas. A thinking person raises a thinking child. That you are even reading this book assures you are a thinking person, so you are on the right track.

Don't expect your child's first grade teacher to stand up in front of the class and say "Okay, it's time to learn to think." Instead, your child's teacher will incorporate activities and language that foster the development and refinement of thinking skills, such as problem solving, concentration, and reasoning, throughout your child's daily activities. In the same way, you will foster thinking skills if you do many of the activities in this book with your child.

There are many approaches to teaching thinking. You can teach your child to use a set of identifiable skills, such as deciding between relevant and irrelevant information and generating questions from written material. This is particularly useful for auditory and visual learners. Your kinesthetic child learns to think more actively by participating in sports, hands-on projects, and similar activities.

Problem Solving

Problem solving is a hallmark of mathematical activity and a major means of developing mathematical knowledge. It is finding a way to reach a goal that is not immediately attainable. Problem solving is natural to young children because the world is new to them, and they exhibit curiosity, intelligence, and flexibility as they face new situations.

The challenge at this level is to build on children's innate problem-solving inclinations and to preserve and encourage a disposition that values problem solving. Try the problem-solving math section in chapter 7 and the science activities about systems in chapter 8 as challenging opportunities for your child.

Concentration

Thinking skills begin with the ability to maintain a focus on one thing long enough to think it through. Thinking something through means understanding the information (in whatever form—for example, visual, print, or oral), questioning the information, and thinking about the alternatives before making a decision.

Concentration skills are a big part of learning to read. Your child's teacher will be working hard with him or her on concentration skills, and you can help reinforce these skills by trying the activities in the reading comprehension section of chapter 5.

Comprehension

This is a hard one. To think about something in a reasonable, logical manner, you need to understand it, but creative thinking is born from instances where you don't understand something. The trick is probably in the mix. Let your child explore new information and form creative thoughts about it, then talk to him or her logically about it. Giving your child time to think freely about new information allows him or her to think about it in many contexts and many forms before being told which concept or form is proper.

In order to better develop your child's understanding of different concepts, his or her perception should be shaped by touching, hearing, and seeing something simultaneously, to experience the concept as best as he or she can. Take time to let your child talk about what he or she is seeing, touching, and hearing. By experiencing new concepts in different contexts, your child can become aware of different aspects of an idea and develop his or her understanding of its meaning.

Reasoning

There is more than one type of reasoning. Formal reasoning skills, such as deductive and inductive reasoning, are developed at a later age. The reasoning skill that is focused on in first grade is spatial-temporal reasoning, or the ability to visualize and transform objects in space.

Spatial-temporal operations are responsible for combining separate elements of an object into a single whole, or for arranging objects in a specific spatial order. Spatial-temporal operations require successive steps; each step is dependent on previous ones.

Spatial-temporal skills are the most frequently tested reasoning/thinking skills on IQ and other standardized tests. You can work on these skills with your child through the math and science activities in this book.

Logic

Children learn about and understand logical concepts in different ways. In math, for example, some kids think about numbers in terms of where they are on a number line, while other kids think about how many objects make up each number. These children reach an understanding of numbers, their meaning, and how to use them, but they reach it in different ways. Taking this example further, these children comprehend the information and understand what numbers represent. But if one group is then asked to handle the numbers in different contexts, the group will need to be aware of different aspects of numbers in order to develop a fuller understanding of their meaning. The group can then think about numbers in different ways and apply them different situations in a logical way rather than simply recall what they mean.

A large part of logical thinking stems from the ability to see objects and apply concepts in many contexts (spatial-temporal reasoning applies here). Teaching children to question information teaches them to think about the information in more than one context before making a logical conclusion about it. Logical thinking can be reinforced during the discipline process by applying logical consequences to a behavior rather than using an arbitrary punishment.

Thinking Skills Activities

To help your child develop thinking skills, you can:

- Encourage her to ask questions about the world around her.

- Ask him to imagine what will happen next in the story when you are reading together.

- Actively listen to your child's conversation, responding seriously and nonjudgmentally to her questions.

- Ask what he is feeling and why when he expresses feelings.

- Suggest that she find facts to support her opinions, and encourage her to locate information relevant to her opinions.

- Use entertainment—a book, a TV program, or a movie—as the basis of family discussions.

- Use daily activities as occasions for learning (environmental learning).

- Reward him for inquisitive and/or creative activity that is productive.

- Ask her what she learned at school.

Environmental Learning

There are thousands of ways that you can use your child's everyday environment to encourage thinking skills. Remember, if your child is an active participant in a home where there are "why" and "how" discussions, he or she is more likely to be an active thinker both in and out of school.

End of First Grade Thinking Skills Checklist

Students who are working at the standard level at the end of first grade:

_____ Shift from learning through observation and experience to learning via language and logic

_____ Demonstrate longer attention spans

_____ Use serious, logical thinking

_____ Are thoughtful and reflective

_____ Are able to understand reasoning and make decisions

Assessment

11

A key component to learning is evaluating what has been learned. Assessment serves several different purposes:

1. Assessing individual student abilities and knowledge and adapting instructions accordingly

2. Evaluating and improving the instructional program in general

3. Determining individual student eligibility for promotion or graduation, college admission, or special honors

4. Measuring and comparing school, school district, statewide, and national performance for broad public accountability

There is more than one kind of assessment and more than one context in which this term is frequently used. There are multiple ways that you and your child's teacher assess your child. There is broad assessment of your child's knowledge of certain things and his performance as compared to other children of the same age and grade. Standardized assessment is usually done at the end of the year and comprises many sessions of test taking in a short time period. There are uses for all types of assessment.

Assessing Individual Student Abilities and Knowledge

Students learn in different ways, so teachers assess their daily learning in different ways. The most common way to assess daily learning is by observing how your child responds to and implements things that he or she learns in the classroom. As teachers observe and consider the variety of daily assignments of students, they begin to help their students demonstrate this learning on tests.

Observation and Portfolio Assessment

Your child's overall progress is assessed by considering her developmental stage and cognitive learning abilities with key concepts and key skills within the framework of her learning styles. Teachers (and by now, you) do this by observing your child on a daily basis, giving basic skills tests, gauging reaction and comprehension time when given new information, and asking frequent, informal questions. All of the activities in this book include explanations for how to assess your child's performance, and the checklists at the beginning and end of the chapters can help you assess your child's progress in each skill.

Teachers have begun to implement portfolio assessment more frequently. Teachers are giving your child the opportunity to demonstrate learning through a variety of activities, such as art projects, writing activities, oral presentations, and daily participation with unit tests, to determine the true levels of comprehension and skill development with the variety of materials and skills in each learning unit. Many people think portfolio assessment is one of the most accurate methods of determining learning, but it can be subjective, so it has been criticized. Teachers try really hard not to be subjective; contrary to what some people think, they aren't likely to retaliate for a mishap with a parent by lowering the child's grades. When a child succeeds, the teacher has also succeeded. Discounting the child's success because of personal feelings destroys the teacher's professional success.

Always remember (even if your child does really well) that achievement tests are just one measure of your child's learning. You know this is true because you have been using rough measures in the activities you do with your child. Observation is a primary assessment tool.

Standardized Testing

Testing is a hot topic, and rightly so. We all remember the standardized tests—spending days filling in little circles with a number 2 pencil.

The majority of teachers dislike standardized testing for a number of reasons. Sure, there is the issue of accountability. But the heart of the issue is not that teachers are afraid of being held to a standard to keep their job—it is that they disagree with being held to what many of them believe is a false standard. Think about how an auditory or physical learner will do on a test designed for visual learners. The tests aren't an accurate picture of what all learners can do.

In defense of test makers, they are doing their best to adjust their approaches within the limitations of state requirements, logistical requirements, and traditional business practices. But the system within which teachers, parents, students, and test makers are trying to operate is definitely imperfect.

Others' issues are centered around "teaching the test." Teachers are afraid the curriculum they are told to teach will be so narrowly geared toward the test that it will limit their ability to teach the things that support the tested items. They are concerned they will only be able to teach to the cognitive learning level when they know the student should also be able to apply the knowledge, synthesize it, and evaluate it. We have discussed how individual scores can be invalid, but so can group scores. Test results may be invalidated by teaching so narrowly to the objectives of a particular test that scores are raised without actually improving the broader, often more important, set of academic skills that the test should be measuring.

At the end of the day, assessment is a very strong tool. It encourages, discourages, and measures learning. Assessment should be a means of fostering growth toward high expectations and should support student learning. When assessments are used in thoughtful and meaningful ways and combined with information from other sources, students' scores provide important information that can lead to decisions that promote student learning and equality of opportunity. The misuse of tests for high-stakes purposes (tests that are used to make significant educational decisions about children, teachers, schools, or school districts) has undermined the benefits these tests can foster.

The standardized tests that cause so much controversy are norm-referenced tests, meaning the test questions are selected so that a national sample of students' test scores will result in a normal distribution: there will always be a group of students at the bottom, a majority in the middle, and a group at the top. It is unrealistic to expect whole groups of students to be in the top percentiles (or groups) on these tests. Most students are expected to perform near the fiftieth percentile.

Helping Your Child Test Well

You play a vital role in helping your child succeed on standardized tests. Here are just a few things you can do:

- Put your child at ease by discussing your own experiences with taking tests. If you were nervous or anxious, talk about it. Let him know those feelings are normal.

- Be aware of the specific days tests will be given. Ask your child how the testing sessions are going. Offer encouragement.

- Stress the importance of listening to test directions and following them carefully. Provide practice activities at home, such as following a recipe or reading and answering questions about a story.

- Make sure your child goes to bed early every night and at the same time every night, especially on the night before testing.

- Encourage healthy eating, rest, and exercise.

- Most standardized testing is given over a three- or four-day period. Ask your child's teacher for a schedule, and make sure your child attends school on those days.

- Meet with your child's teachers to discuss the results. If your child had difficulty in specific areas, ask teachers for suggestions in the form of homework assignments, techniques, and specific material.

What the Scores Really Mean

High-stakes tests are used to make significant educational decisions about children, teachers, schools, or school districts. To use a single objective test in the determination of such things as graduation, course credit, grade placement, promotion to the next grade, or placement in special groups is a serious misuse of tests. Remember, your child's score on a standardized test is only one measure of what he knows. Most schools use multiple measures, including student projects, homework, portfolios, chapter tests, and oral reports.

Measuring and Comparing School, School District, Statewide, and National Performance for Broad Public Accountability

Increasingly, policy makers at the federal, state, and local levels want to identify ways to measure student performance in order to see how well the public education system is doing its job. The goals of this account-ability approach include providing information about the status of the educational system, motivating desired change, measuring program effectiveness, and creating systems for rewarding and sanctioning educators based on the performance of their students.

The use of testing to change classroom instruction is central to the theory of standards-based reform. It assumes that educators and the public can agree on what should be taught; that a set of clear standards can be developed, which in turn drive curriculum and instruction; and that tests can measure how well students perform based on those standards.

First Grade Society 12

First graders are social little people. They spend time with lots of different kids, as well as adults, all day every day. This chapter discusses certain aspects of social growth and changes that first graders encounter. It is by no means inclusive of every social issue that your child may face, but it will give you a basis to understand and help your child make the most of exciting social growth while successfully navigating some potentially choppy waters.

Groups

During the past two or three years your child has gone from being "yours" to being a soccer, tee ball, or basketball player; a member of a class and a school; a Sunday school or Hebrew school student; a scout; and so on. This is the year that good citizenship at school and in the community has become the focus in social studies. Your child has probably become hyperaware of the groups that he or she is a member of and the behavior expected to remain a member in good standing.

Identifying with a group is a good, healthy developmental sign. It must, however, be kept in check throughout your child's life, and the earlier this starts the better. You can look for these signs that may indicate your child could use a little help interacting with groups of children in a healthy, appropriate manner:

- He excludes nonmembers consistently.
- She excludes nonmembers in a mean way.
- He has excessive anxiety over group activities.
- She has unrealistic expectations of group members.
- He tries to exert inappropriate control in group activities.

Children sometimes use group situations as a way to explore power, ownership, and control: "You can't sit here! This is our table!" This behavior indicates your child is on the road to bullydom, and you should start intervening right away. Don't be afraid to step into her social scenario. There are several ways you can respond:

- Acknowledge the activity that is already going on. As you describe to children what you see them doing and ask them to talk about it, they will start feeling less threatened and more confident that their play will be able to continue if a new person is introduced: "The two of you have been working hard over here. Can you tell Shondra and me what you are building?" In many cases, when kids understand that the new person won't threaten their play, they allow her to join.

- Talk with your child about ways the new person could join. You can offer a suggestion: "So, this is a fire station. Do you need someone to bring water for the fire? I wonder if Jake could help you with that." Or you can ask children for their ideas: "What kinds of workers does a fire station need? Is there a way Lisa could help with the fire station?" Or, "Travis, do you have an idea of something you could do in the fire station?"

- Establish limits to prevent children from being physically or emotionally hurt. You can set ground rules to help them be nice: "I won't allow you to say that to Leila. It hurts feelings when you call people names. Let's figure out another way to tell her your idea. You could say, 'I just want to play with Sara right now. Maybe I could play with you later.'"

- Find ways to challenge exclusions based on your child's categorical thinking. It is important that we don't allow children to treat somebody hurtfully based on their membership in a particular group. As well as stopping children from excluding someone because she is a girl or because he has a "funny nose," it is important to challenge children's thinking. You can do this by asking children to think about behavior rather than physical characteristics: "So what do you need to be able to do to play here?" Once kids have outlined the necessary skills, you can talk with the person who wants to join about which of those things she might be able to do: "Julie says that she loves to dig. She could help you make your hole deeper." If children "require" skills that the new child doesn't possess, you can help them broaden their thinking by offering other ideas for help: "Darren isn't tall enough to build on the top there, but he could bring carpet pieces for the floor."

Independence Day

It can be hard to let go—or not. It is particularly not hard to let go when your child is lunging away from you with full body weight. He is testing to see how far the boundaries really expand with each age and grade: "Can I stay up until nine-thirty when I am in third grade? Can I do that when I am seven? Do first graders ride their bikes to school?" So get ready to hear (if you haven't already), "I am in first grade now, so I should be able to walk to the bus stop myself." Your child may have been asking to ride his bike past your street or maybe he will wear only clothes that he picks out himself.

You are noticing your child becoming more independent on an almost daily basis, and it is scary. How do children go from two months to twenty years in warp speed? School is how. Socially they are full-time members of a community with daily behavior and performance expectations in addition to academic issues. Children assimilate very quickly, and you will notice a huge difference in your first grader's behavior. This is great and totally normal.

If your child is being homeschooled, it is essential that you incorporate into your homeschool curriculum community-based activities that promote independence. Increase your expectations of your child's social behaviors and set a routine that you adhere to at all times. A big part of school centers on spending the day in a productive fashion while being a kind and thoughtful member of a community. It is difficult to teach concepts such as being a good neighbor, sharing, and reasons for rules and consequences for breaking them to children if they are not members of a community of peers.

If your child seems to be having trouble stepping out into the world, try helping by:

- Assuring him it is okay to be afraid, but sometimes the things you like best are the things you used to be afraid of

- Enrolling him in one or two after-school activities (but not too many—let him focus and succeed)

My Best Friend

As a child (and as an adult) your best friend is your comrade in arms, your soul sister, your security blanket. Having a best friend makes it easier to become a part of new situations.

Your first grade child is still trying to understand what friendships are and how they work. There are periods during the first five years when children think they can have only one friend at a time; when they're playing with one friend, they tend to exclude a third person who wants to play. Even though your six- or seven-year-old is emerging from this way of thinking, she still categorizes friendships. For example, she may have a best friend at school (and that can change from year to year or month to month!), a best friend at home or in the neighborhood, a best friend at church, a best friend at soccer, and so on. Your child will probably have a "best-best" friend, but by and large she will categorize friendships (as many adults do) by activity, place, or convenience. The basic rules of first grade friendships are:

- They often fall into categories.

- They are volatile—feelings can get hurt and mended easily.

- Distance does not make the heart grow fonder—it is more like out of sight, out of mind.

- They are the basis for your child's success at forming and maintaining a variety of friendships in later life.

- They can be formed through healthy (common interests) or unhealthy (excluding others) events.

Categorizing friendships is not necessarily a bad thing. It is a healthy developmental stage, but be careful. It is important to make the effort with your child to foster friendships that are "outside the box," even if it means a thirty-five-minute drive across town. If you and your child limit yourselves to friendships that are convenient, it is likely you are also limiting your exposure and your child's to new and different experiences. Here are some tips for helping your child broaden her base of friendships:

- *Intramural sports*: Sport teams that are sponsored by your local parks and recreation league are more diverse than those that are neighborhood based.

- *Classes*: Swimming, art, gymnastics, dance, computers—any kind of class that interests your child is a good place to find potential friends with similar interests.

- *Volunteering*: It is never too early to teach your child that public service is a good way to meet nice people while helping the community. Depending on where you live, you will find activities such as cleaning a park or beach, planting flowers, visiting seniors, collecting food for the needy, and so forth. They are easy to find and rewarding in many ways.

No, You Can't Play!

No matter how many best friends your child has, no matter how popular he is, and no matter how well behaved, your child is likely to have some kind of issue that revolves around the playground. He has recess one to three times a day, and if you haven't dealt with playground problems yet, you are about to. It is the time of day when children are given a break from close adult supervision, and that means there is greater chance for conflicts to arise.

The most common playground problem is one child being excluded from playing with others. This can lead to children defining roles for themselves such as bully and victim. If you suspect that your child has taken on either of these, get to the root of the problem now and talk with him about how to handle the situation. Children exclude others for many reasons. With beginning-level social skills, they sometimes end up playing with a friend without knowing how they got there, how the play started, or how to get the play going again in the future. The friendship may seem tenuous to them, and any little distraction can feel like it threatens the continuation of their activity.

Children also exclude others because they are too concrete (remember Piaget?) to conceptualize playing with more than one "type" of friend at once. Many times children play a different role with different people. Your child may act one way with you, another with brothers and sisters, and still another with Grandma. Your child easily categorizes her behavior with friends. For example, she may play dress-up with one friend and make forts with another friend. Trying to play with both of these friends at once may be confusing—she doesn't know how to be the dress-up self and the fort-builder self at the same time. This is a developmental stage that children simply must outgrow. If your child is excluded from a play date with one of her friends and you suspect this is the reason, comfort her and divert her attention to another activity. Try arranging for the children to play at a later date when your child and her friend can play one on one.

Children at this developmental stage have difficulty being flexible. If your child is intent on joining playmates who are trying to exclude her, then you can arm her with these tricks:

- Teach your child to compliment the other kids on their play: "That is a cool fort. How did you build it?"

- Teach your child to think of a way to contribute to the activity so that the other kids can see she can have a role: "Are you playing house? I have a tea set. Can I be the sister who serves tea?" Or, "Can I help build that sand castle? I am really good at digging."

- Teach your child to ask for help: "I have been trying to hit a ball without a tee [transitioning from tee ball to softball]. Can you show me how to do it?"

- Talk to your child about knowing when to walk away and let the other kids play. No one likes a needy person—even at six or seven. Part of the trick to playing with others in a fun way is also knowing how to entertain yourself.

If you find that your child is being particularly choosy about who she plays with, ask why. She may have a valid reason for not playing with certain children.

Moving On to Second Grade

You made it! Your first grader is now going to be a second grader, and you are going to be the parent of a second grader!

You can monitor your child's readiness for second grade and determine areas that you can help your child reinforce with the following subject area and developmental checklists.

Ready to Go

Students who are ready to go on to second grade:

Reading

____ Develop appropriate active strategies to construct meaning from print

____ Decode unfamiliar words

____ Understand how speech sounds are connected

____ Understand or are able to figure out (using contextual clues) the meaning of what they read

____ Develop and maintain motivation to read

____ Extend a story

_____ Predict what will happen next

_____ Discuss the characters' motives

_____ Question the author's meaning

_____ Describe causes and effects of events in the text

_____ Discuss books by tying their comments directly to the text

Writing

_____ Communicate in writing

_____ Reread their writing to monitor meaning

_____ Begin to use feedback to change their writing, either by adding more text or by making minor revisions

_____ Insert text in the middle of their writing rather than just at the end

_____ Make deliberate choices about the language they use

_____ Use punctuation and capitalization more often than not

Math

_____ Work with patterns and sequences

_____ Add and subtract single-digit numbers

_____ Tell time

_____ Count money

_____ Identify place values to hundreds

_____ Practice measuring length, capacity, and weight

_____ Work with geometric shapes

_____ Become familiar with the concept of symmetry

_____ Count higher than 100

_____ Understand fractions

_____ Solve simple word problems

Science

____ Identify and describe bodies of water and marine life

____ Make observations and recognize similarities and differences

____ Categorize living and nonliving things and systems

____ Understand that there are a variety of earth materials

____ Describe life stages, particularly of a butterfly or a tadpole

Social Studies

____ Know the name of their country

____ Know the name of their state

____ Know and follow school and community rules

____ Understand there are places with special meaning to people, usually called landmarks

____ Name and understand the meanings behind major U.S. holidays

Thinking

____ Shift from learning through observation and experience to learning via language and logic

Demonstrate a longer attention span

____ Use serious, logical thinking; are thoughtful and reflective

____ Are able to understand reasoning and make the right decisions

Anxieties

There are always going to be anxieties when moving on to another grade. After all, you just got to know the first grade teacher and you really like her. Who will be the homeroom mom next year? Wait—this is supposed to be about the children's anxieties, right? Wrong.

Everyone is going to feel a little sad, a little anxious, a little excited, and really glad it is summer when the subject of second grade arises.

If your child's teacher has recommended that your child be held back for a year, don't spend an excessive amount of time worrying. Kindergarten and first grade are the most appropriate times to hold a child back. Developmental growth is the most disparate at this age and is most easily corrected and brought up to grade level by reteaching the first grade building blocks as your child's cognitive and developmental growth enables him to fully grasp them. The absolute worst thing you can do is fight this.

The way you handle your child repeating a grade will factor into his self-esteem for a lifetime. Do not be embarrassed, do not be ashamed, and do not assume your child is "slow." Your child needs extra time to develop skills that come with growth. Give him that time and the self-esteem that he deserves.

Minimizing "Brain Drain"

Now that your child has acquired tangible skills that are building blocks for future learning, you are facing your first year of the challenge of keeping those skills fresh. Here are some things to keep in mind to help your child retain his or her first grade skills during the summer months.

Do

- Reinforce skills from his or her first grade year through environmental learning.

- Go to the library on a regular basis.

- Include learning activities in your weekly summer routine.

- Encourage free and creative thinking through art projects or active play.

Don't

- Try to "get ahead" for the next year.

- Have your child spend the whole summer with a tutor.

- Ignore obvious learning opportunities (such as mapping out the trip to Grandma's).

Your child's first grade year has been enhanced, supported, and furthered by your efforts. Continue creating the learning environment that you worked so hard on this year over the summer and into second grade. You are on the right track.

LITERATURE FOR FIRST GRADERS

This section contains a list of books that your child may find interesting and learning activities along with the reading selections. You can find more recommended literature for your first grader at www. knowledgeessentials.com.

Danny and the Dinosaur

Author: Syd Hoff

Publisher: Harper Trophy

This book is about a little boy who meets a dinosaur in the museum. They leave the museum to have a fun day of adventures. This book is part of a series by the author.

Special Considerations: Parents may need to help with words such as "dinosaur" and "museum," but children should be able to read this one quickly on their own.

Learning: Look up facts about dinosaurs. Talk about reality versus fantasy and fact versus fiction. Is *Danny and the Dinosaur* fact or fiction?

Activity: Let your child draw a dinosaur. Ask him to write a sentence about the drawing. Have him read the sentence aloud and post the picture on the refrigerator or on a bulletin board.

Follow Up: Visit a local museum. Continue talking about reality versus fantasy and fact versus fiction.

Frog and Toad Are Friends
Author: Arnold Lobel
Publisher: HarperCollins

This book has five short stories about a frog and a toad that become friends and learn lessons together.

Special Considerations: This is a chapter book—it is probably a little longer than those your child is able to read on her own. Practice reading it together or give your child a bookmark to stop at each chapter.

Learning: Find facts about frogs and toads. How are they similar? How are they different?

Activity: Research the life cycle of a frog together. What are the stages that a tadpole goes through to become a frog? Ask your child to draw a picture of each stage.

Follow Up: Use a piece of stationery and an envelope to write a letter to a friend or relative. Show your child how to address the envelope, and put the letter in the mail together.

Harry and the Lady Next Door
Author: Arnold Lobel
Publisher: HarperCollins

Harry the dog gets into trouble when he tries to get his neighbor the opera singer to stop singing. This book is part of a popular series.

Special Considerations: Your child should be able to read this on his own after practicing some of the harder words with you.

Learning: Talk about being a good citizen and a good neighbor. What would your child do if his neighbor was like Harry's? Tell your child about the ways grown-ups might handle the situation.

Activity: Listen to your child's favorite song. Sing and write the words.

Follow Up: Check out a tape from a different genre than you usually listen to (show music, opera, orchestra). Talk about the different types of music.

Eloise
Author: Kay Thompson
Publisher: Simon & Schuster

Eloise is a model of self-confidence who lives at New York City's Plaza Hotel. "Getting bored is not allowed," so she fills her days to the brim with adventures and self-imposed responsibilities.

Special Considerations: This book is written in a conversational style that mimics language use of a six-year-old. This series is an excellent way to talk about a variety of settings while using maps and globes.

Learning: This is another good opportunity to talk about fact versus fiction. What parts of the story talk about things or places that are real? What parts of the story talk about things or places that are made up?

Activity: Go to the library and locate fiction and nonfiction books. Check out two fiction books and two nonfiction books.

Follow Up: Talk about the setting of the book. Locate New York on a map. Locate New York City and, if possible, Manhattan. Talk about the Plaza Hotel and where it is in New York (in Manhattan at the southeastern side of Central Park). Why is the hotel a good setting for a book?

Bedtime for Frances

Author: Russell Hoban
Publisher: Viking Press

Frances the badger can't go to sleep. She takes her parents through the gamut—from delay tactics to urgent requests to fearing strange noises and scary shapes. This is part of a sixties-era series of children's books about a family of badgers.

Special Considerations: Your child should be able to read this book alone, but the story is a good one to read together.

Learning: Use this story as an opportunity to talk about what things are important to keep us healthy and how our bodies need sleep. What happens when you don't get enough sleep or eat the right things? What are the food groups and how many servings of each should you eat? What is a proper serving?

Activity: Find a picture of the food pyramid. Draw the outline of a pyramid for your child and label the types of foods that should go in each part of the pyramid. Ask her to draw the kinds of foods that she likes in the appropriate part of the pyramid.

Follow Up: Make a list of the things your child is going to do the next day. Ask her which things can be changed and which things can't be changed. What would change if your child didn't get enough sleep? Would she be able to play as long the next day? How can you tell if people are tired? Do they act differently?

Clifford the Big Red Dog

Author: Norman Bridwell
Publisher: Scholastic

Clifford is an enormous dog whose size is always a problem. He is so big that his house is bigger than his owner's house, and he gets a bath in the swimming pool. This book is part of a series that has been around for over thirty-five years and became a popular animated TV series.

Special Considerations: There may be some confusing letter pairs for beginning readers, but your child will be able to read most of this book on his own.

Learning: It is a good jumping-off point for a discussion of comparative words, superlatives, and endings. List all of the comparative words that you and your child can think of (for example, big, bigger, biggest; tall, taller, tallest). Underline the root words in one color, the -er endings in another color, and the -est endings in a third color.

Activity: Ask your child to draw something in all three forms of one of the sets of comparative words that you have listed.

Follow Up: Look up three different breeds of dogs and learn about their characteristics.

If You Give a Mouse a Cookie
Author: Laura Numeroff
Publisher: Laura Geringer Books/HarperCollins

"If you give a mouse a cookie, he will want a glass of milk to go with it." This is a great book to show in a funny way that there are consequences for every action and what happens when you want too much.

Special Considerations: There are a couple of words that may be challenging, such as "blanket" or "comfortable," but your child should be able to read most of this book on her own.

Learning: Have you ever wanted more than you can have? Explain that most people have unlimited wants for goods and services—the list of things they want never ends. Make a list of things your child wants.

Can she have them all? How do you decide what to have and what not to have?

Activity: Explain that the mouse had many wants. Some of the things the mouse wanted were goods. Goods are things the mouse could touch and use. For example, the mouse wanted a cookie. A cookie is a good. Ask your child to name other goods the mouse wanted (milk, broom, scissors, straw, napkin, mop, bucket, box, pillow, paper, crayon, pen, tape). Explain that not all the things the mouse wanted were goods. One thing was a service: the mouse wanted the boy to read a story. A service is something someone does for you.

Follow Up: Brainstorm a list of services that your child sees performed in everyday life. Ask your child to draw a picture of a service that she sees performed every day.

Henry and Mudge: The First Book of Their Adventure
Author: Cynthia Rylant
Publisher: Aladdin Library

This is the story of Henry, a little boy with no one to play with until he finds Mudge, a 180-pound dog. He and Mudge turn everyday life into a lot of fun together.

Special Considerations: This book is readable by first graders at the end of the year. If reading it sooner, you may want to read it to your child.

Learning: Talk about dogs as pets but also as service or working dogs. What services do dogs help people perform? (Seeing eye dogs, police dogs, ranch or farm dogs.)

Activity: Look at pictures of dogs. Talk about different breeds of dogs. Pick out one or two breeds and list the characteristics. Ask your child to draw a picture of each. Ask him to write a fact about the dogs he chose.

Follow Up: Learn some safety tips about dogs, such as never petting a strange dog.

Green Eggs and Ham
Author: Dr. Seuss
Publisher: Random House

Children love the funny rhymes and repetition in this classic story of Sam I Am, the picky eater who won't try a new food.

Special Considerations: This is a good book for beginning readers to master reading on their own.

Learning: Rhymes are a fun way to reinforce phonics. Talk about what sounds the letters make and which ones rhyme. What makes a rhyme? Make up rhymes on your own.

Activity: Pick out a couple of simple recipes and let your child select one to make. Read the recipe together. Let her gather ingredients by sight and by reading labels. Follow the directions on the recipe together.

Follow Up: Sequencing is a good follow-up concept. What happened first, second, and third in the book? When you were making the recipe together, what did you do first, second, and third?

Are You My Mother?
Author: P. D. Eastman
Publisher: Random House

A little bird hatches while his mother is out searching for food. He goes in search of her without knowing what she looks like, creating funny and sweet situations.

Special Considerations: Your first grader should be able to read this on his own.

Learning: Talk about offspring and parents and how heredity means they look mostly alike.

Activity: Write an animal on an index card and the name of that animal's baby on another index card (for example, cow, calf; chicken, chick). Let your child match them.

Follow Up: Brainstorm a list of animals. Talk about the names of the offspring. Research the animals whose offspring you can't name. Find the answers together. Researching answers together helps demonstrate to your child that answers to questions can be found, and that no matter how smart you are, it is important to know where to find information.

SOFTWARE FOR FIRST GRADERS

Are you eager to use your computer as a learning tool? I bet you told yourself that educational software is the real reason you needed to get the upgraded media package. Here is the chance to redeem yourself. This appendix provides a list of software titles that are appropriate and interesting for first grade learners. Since your child may be more adept at the technical portion of the activity, it is not listed. If all else fails, refer to the software's user guide. You can find more recommended computer resources for your first grader at www.knowledgeessentials.com.

Reader Rabbit 1st Grade
Broderbund

This software covers basic first grade math, reading, writing, and spelling skills. Players try to win the games to collect the missing stage props so that a big variety show can go on as planned. The level of difficulty of each game automatically adjusts to your child's progress.

Product Focus: First grade basic skill sets.

The Living Sea
Montparnasse Multimedia

Fish fans will love learning about the ocean and biology with this program. Most of the activities focus on facts about the sea, but there are also thinking skills and art activities.

Product Focus: First grade science concepts.

JumpStart Advanced 1st Grade
Knowledge Adventure

This software is broken up into three sections: Fundamentals, Music, and Art Club. Children are assigned a guide that takes them through all of the activities and gives hints if they get stuck. There is also a feature that allows you to check on your child's progress.

Product Focus: First grade basic skill sets.

Big Thinkers First Grade
Humongous Entertainment

The guides for this program become the activities. They turn themselves into trains, cranes, and clocks as children learn about fractions and how to tell time. Other activities include reading, art, and science. Parents are able to track the child's development on the program.

Product Focus: First grade basic skill sets and science concepts.

Madeline Classroom Companion 1st and 2nd Grade
Creative Wonders

Children go shopping on Main Street with Madeline, the character from the classic story. They learn math, grammar, and beginning French and Spanish. The set includes first and second grade activities.

Product Focus: First grade basic skill sets.

Math Blaster for 1st Grade
Knowledge Adventure

This is like an arcade game that teaches children math. Children travel through space with their alien guides and solve problems in order to clean up a mess made by the Trash Alien.

Product Focus: First grade math concepts.

Carmen Sandiego Junior Detective Edition
Broderbund

Children help Carmen Sandiego fight crime. Kids use clues to track criminals all over the world. Geography and map skills are used throughout the game along with thinking and reasoning.

Product Focus: First grade social studies concepts and thinking skills.

Magic School Bus Series
Microsoft

Ms. Frizzle, the teacher from the cartoon and books, leads adventures that teach a variety of subjects and reinforce a variety of skills. Most children like being able to interact with Ms. Frizzle, and there are a variety of titles available.

Product Focus: First grade basic skill sets.

Math Missions Grades K–2: The Race to Spectacle City Arcade
Scholastic

Children use math skills to earn money to get to the arcade. Every time your child completes an activity, she earns money to play fun games in the arcade.

Product Focus: First grade math concepts.

Powerpuff Girls: Mojo Jojo's Clone Zone
Learning Challenge 1

Children work with the Powerpuff Girls to fight the clones. They use their math, vocabulary, and reading skills to help the girls save Townsville.

Product Focus: First grade basic skill sets.

Lego Racers
Lego

Kids get to build and race Lego cars through a variety of racetracks. They can also design the driver and select a driving style. The software introduces and reinforces basic engineering and spatial visualization skills.

Product Focus: First grade math and thinking skills.

FIRST GRADE TOPICAL CALENDAR

This calendar tells you approximately when the skills covered in this book occur during the school year. There will be variances, of course, but for the most part the skills build on one another, so it is logical that your child will learn things in a certain order.

Reading	Writing	Math	Science and Social Studies
September			
Rhyming words	Writing process: forming letters, words, and sentences	Graphing	(Intro to these topics)
Blends		Matching	Weather
Comprehension		Sorting	Living/nonliving
Parts of a book			Mothers and babies
			Scientific method
			School rules
October			
Parts of speech: nouns and verbs	Writing process: forming letters, words, and sentences	Even and odd	Fall
Comprehension		Skip counting	Fish
		Comparing sizes	Magnets, magnifying glass
			Community
			Wants and needs

Reading	Writing	Math	Science and Social Studies
November			
Word families	Sentences	Addition	Holidays
Vocabulary		Subtraction	Birds
Comprehension		Matching numerals to the words	Classify and describe
December			
Main idea	Punctuation	Simple word problems	Holidays
Comprehension			Cultures
Extending a story			Families
January			
Fiction and nonfiction	Descriptive words	Measurement	Winter
Comprehension		Telling time	Birds
			Classify and describe
February			
Characters	Descriptive words	Place value	Habitats
Setting	Paragraphs	Sets	Things necessary to live
Comprehension			
March			
Syllables	The writing process	Counting money	Spring
Fantasy			Plants
Realistic fiction			
Comprehension			
April			
Syllables	The writing process	Fractions	Things that live in the earth
			Earth materials
May			
Independent reading	The writing process	Application of skills	Summer
			The life cycle of a butterfly

GLOSSARY

accountability Holding students responsible for what they learn and teachers responsible for what they teach.

achievement test A test designed to efficiently measure the amount of knowledge and/or skill a person has acquired. This helps evaluate student learning in comparison with a standard or norm.

assessment Measuring a student's learning.

authentic assessment The concept of model, practice, and feedback in which students know what excellent performance is and are guided to practice an entire concept rather than bits and pieces in preparation for eventual understanding.

benchmark A standard by which student performance can be measured in order to compare it with and improve one's own skills or learning.

Bloom's taxonomy A classification system for learning objectives that consists of six levels ranging from knowledge (which focuses on the reproduction of facts) to evaluation (which represents higher-level thinking).

competency test A test intended to determine whether a student has met established minimum standards of skills and knowledge and is thus eligible for promotion, graduation, certification, or other official acknowledgment of achievement.

concept An abstract, general notion—a heading that characterizes a set of behaviors and beliefs.

content goals Statements that are like learning standards or learning objectives, but which only describe the topics to be studied, not the skills to be performed.

criterion-referenced test A test in which the results can be used to determine a student's progress toward mastery of a content area or designated objectives of an instructional program. Performance is compared to an expected level of mastery in a content area rather than to other students' scores.

curriculum The content and skills that are taught at each grade level.

curriculum alignment The connection of subjects across grade levels, cumulatively, to build comprehensive, increasingly complex instructional programs.

high-stakes testing Any testing program whose results have important consequences for students, teachers, colleges, and/or areas, such as promotion, certification, graduation, or denial/approval of services and opportunity.

IQ test A psychometric test that scores the performance of certain intellectual tasks and can provide assessors with a measurement of general intelligence.

learning objectives A set of expectations that are needed to meet the learning standard.

learning standards Broad statements that describe what content a student should know and what skills a student should be able to demonstrate in different subject areas.

measurement Quantitative description of student learning and qualitative description of student attitude.

median   The point on a scale that divides a group into two equal subgroups. The median is not affected by low or high scores as is the mean. (See also **norm**.)

metacognition   The knowledge of one's own thinking processes and strategies, and the ability to consciously reflect and act on the knowledge of cognition to modify those processes and strategies.

multiple-choice test   A test in which students are presented with a question or an incomplete sentence or idea. The students are expected to choose the correct or best answer or completion from a menu of alternatives.

norm   A distribution of scores obtained from a norm group. The norm is the midpoint (or median) of scores or performance of the students in that group. Fifty percent will score above the norm and 50 percent will score below it.

norm group   A random group of students selected by a test developer to take a test to provide a range of scores and establish the percentiles of performance for use in determining scoring standards.

norm-referenced test   A test in which a student or a group's performance is compared to that of a norm group. The results are relative to the performance of an external group and are designed to be compared with the norm group, resulting in a performance standard. These tests are often used to measure and compare students, schools, districts, and states on the basis of norm-established scales of achievement.

outcome   An operationally defined educational goal, usually a culminating activity, product, or performance that can be measured.

performance-based assessment   Direct observation and rating of student performance of an educational objective, often an ongoing observation over a period of time, and typically involving the creation of products dealing with real life. Performance-based assessments use performance criteria to determine the degree to which a student has met an achievement target. Important elements of performance-based assessment include clear goals or performance criteria clearly articulated and communicated to the learner.

performance goals   Statements that are like learning standards or learning objectives, but they only describe the skills to be performed, not the content to be studied.

portfolio assessment   A systematic and organized collection of a student's work that exhibits to others the direct evidence of a student's efforts, achievements, and progress over a period of time. The collection should involve the student in selection of its contents and should include information about the performance criteria, the rubric or criteria for judging merit, and evidence of student self-relocation or evaluation. It should include representative work, providing documentation of the learner's performance and a basis for evaluation of the student's progress. Portfolios may include a variety of demonstrations of learning.

BIBLIOGRAPHY

Bloom, B. S. (ed.) (1956). *Taxonomy of Educational Objectives: The Classification of Educational Goals: Handbook I, Cognitive Domain.* New York: Longmans, Green.

Brainerd, C. J. (1978). *Piaget's Theory of Intelligence.* New Jersey: Prentice Hall, Inc.

Evans, R. (1973). *Jean Piaget: The Man and His Ideas.* New York: E. P. Dutton & Co., Inc.

Lavatelli, C. (1973). *Piaget's Theory Applied to an Early Childhood Curriculum.* Boston: American Science and Engineering, Inc.

London, C. (1988). "A Piagetian constructivist perspective on curriculum development." *Reading Improvement 27,* 82–95.

Piaget, J. (1972). "Development and Learning." In Lavatelli, C. S., and Stendler, F. *Reading in Child Behavior and Development.* New York: Harcourt Brace Janovich.

——— (1972). *To Understand Is to Invent.* New York: The Viking Press, Inc.

Shure, M. B. (1993). *Interpersonal Problem Solving and Prevention: A Comprehensive Report of Research and Training.* A five-year longitudinal study, Kindergarten through grade 4, no. MH-40801. Washington, D.C.: National Institute of Mental Health.

Shure, M. B., and G. Spivack (1980). "Interpersonal Problem Solving as a Mediator of Behavioral Adjustment in Preschool and Kindergarten Children." *Journal of Applied Developmental Psychology 1* 29–44.

——— (1982). "Interpersonal Problem-solving in Young Children: A Cognitive Approach to Prevention." *American Journal of Community Psychology 10,* 341–356.

Sigel, I., and R. Cocking (1977). *Cognitive Development from Childhood to Adolescence: A Constructivist Perspective.* New York: Holt, Rinehart and Winston.

Singer, D., and T. Revenson (1978). *A Piaget Primer: How a Child Thinks.* New York: International Universities Press, Inc.

Willis, Mariaemma, and Victoria Hodson (1999). *Discover Your Child's Learning Style.* New York: Crown Publishing Group.

INDEX